IT'S YOUR LIFE
IT'S YOUR CHOICE

CREATE TOMORROW'S SUCCESSES
TODAY

by Chris Demetriou

First published by ACTS International Corp. In 2012.

ISBN 978-0-9557280-4-4

Table of Contents

I dedicate this book to all the people who are still on the road of discovery. May your steps be ordered and your path straight, and may you find God's plan and purpose for your life and fulfil your destiny.

Introduction

"Life is a sum of all your choices."

Albert Camus

Guided by the belief that today's choices create tomorrow's successes, I decided to write a book that carefully separated the different components of what it takes to make "right" choices. To excel in your chosen field and find lasting satisfaction in doing so, you will need to understand your unique patterns and how they effect the choices you make. To nurture success, you will also need to practice and refine a positive mental attitude. In some ways, I was never sure how it all came together until I sat down to write this book. I was able to shift my focus and explore the intricate detail of what is required to make the right choices in life. I am now convinced that the true path to success is through the application of timeless principles supported by the solid foundation of personal character.

Over the past three decades I have managed to sustain an unusual measure of success. Some of the time this was unintentional.

Many may think my life's experiences are what dreams are made of. I wrote my first hit song at the age of sixteen, and after moving to London I worked with some of the world's greatest recording artists. When I left the music industry and got involved in other business opportunities, many worthwhile accomplishments followed. Most of these achievements came about because I was able to identify new possibilities and create the right environment for those possibilities to materialise into commercially viable ventures. Whatever skills and abilities I may have developed, my life's achievements can probably be attributed to making the right choices – whether intentionally or unintentionally. If you think about it, your life is much the same. It is a rambling collection of all your choices, some good and others quite foolish.

The choices you make today frame your tomorrows

Choices are building blocks for every future accomplishment. Therefore, you can create tomorrow's successes today. This book has been written to help you choose "right" in every situation, regardless of negative circumstances. It comes in two parts. Part one, THE LAW OF CONSTRUCTIVE CHOICE, looks at seven distinct character traits. These are useful attributes you are encouraged to embrace if you are to make right choices. The Law of Constructive Choice is centred round the understanding that productive and beneficial choices stem directly from a positive temperament that has been established through correct knowledge of 'self'. Part two, THE LAW OF EFFECTIVE CHOICE, examines seven specific things you must "choose" in order to create a dynamic, balanced and fulfilled life. This law says – *"make the right choices and you'll get the right results."* It's that simple!

As you examine the following chapters, I'd like you to keep in mind three ideas:

1. The ability to choose right can be learned. Some of the principles outlined are easier to understand than others, but every one of them can be acquired and implemented.

2. Each principle compliments all the others. However, you don't need one in order to learn another.

3. Choices carry consequences. Choose right and your future is secure, but ignore these principles and you will pay the price.

The ability to make right choices is a skill

The ability to make the right choices is one of the most important skills you can learn. It is a critical factor that enables you to take command of every situation and use it to your benefit. The good news is that you can learn to make the right choices. You can be taught how to set a direction or course in life that will move you toward fulfilment and true happiness. The first step is to change the way you think. Mary Engelbreit said, *"If you don't like something change it; if you can't change it, change the way you think about it."*

Change yourself and gain control of your life

To be in control of your life you have to consciously choose to change and to keep changing yourself to become the very person you want to be. All change starts with a change of mind, and you start by changing your thoughts about the things you want to alter, adjust or transform. In changing the way you think you immediately change your perception and consequently the way you feel about it.

When you change the way you feel about something, you change your behaviour, and this is how you make progress and grow. Constantly trying to change your behaviour will rarely create long term and lasting change, but when you change your mind-set the rest will follow. If you never change then you simply can't grow and if you don't grow you are not developing your potential or exploiting your true capabilities.

To change your life for the better and pave the way for success you need to grow systematically (making progress in key areas). However, in doing so you must learn to make things easier for yourself. You must aim to achieve decisive change but do it with the least possible effort. Changing your 'view' of something is probably the easiest and most beneficial way you can effect positive change, and this involves exercising your freedom of choice. Freedom of choice is an amazing thing. It is one of the most fundamental freedoms there is, and it should be much appreciated.

Freedom can be defined as *"the absence of necessity, coercion, or constraint in choice of action."* But for freedom of choice to achieve anything, there must exist the possibility of making a choice between many different alternatives. This implies variety and abundance but it's variety and abundance perceived by your mind.

Freedom of choice is everything

People with limiting beliefs, restrictive patterns and bad habits suppress their freedom of choice because their view of life is narrow and one dimensional. I was like that at one time in my life. My beliefs were all self centred and my negative habits were bordering on being compulsive. I was unable to effectively exercise my freedom of choice because my view of life was extremely narrow, and therefore, I always ended up choosing the quick fix or pursuing the soft option. I very rarely saw any viable alternatives. However, in order to implement beneficial changes you must have genuine alternatives, and your perception of these alternatives must be realistic when exercising your free will. If your alternatives are based on assumptions or speculation then the decisions you make will be unreliable. Being realistic and clear about your choices accounts for 80 percent of the success and happiness you create.

Lack of clarity is probably more responsible for frustration and underachievement than any other single factor. Your success in life will be largely determined by how realistic and clear you are about what it is you really want. The more realistic and clear you are about your desires, the more likely you are to do more and more of the things that are consistent with achieving them. As a result, you will do fewer and fewer things that don't help you to get what you really want.

This applies to choices as well. The clearer and more realistic you are about your choices, the more effective you will be in deciding which alternative to take. And as a result, you will move quicker toward your goals.

Ideas are a mode of transportation

Every advance you make begins with a single idea – a single thought. It is the fresh ideas you generate daily that will enable you to solve problems, overcome obstacles, and achieve your goals. Ideas are keys to the future, and I expect your mind to be flooded with new ideas as you read this book. Remember, it's not possible for you to achieve anything in life except to the degree to which you think creatively. Ideas are a mode of transportation – you can use them to take you wherever you want to go.

There is virtually no obstacle in life that you cannot overcome with the power of creative thought. It's not what happens to you but how you think about what happens to you that will determine how you feel and react. It is not the world outside you that dictates your circumstances or conditions. It is the world inside you that creates the conditions of your life, and this is fundamentally a creative process. Having started my professional life as a musician and songwriter I became very familiar with this creative process. The world inside of me determined what I would write, create or produce. Therefore, this creative process motivated me and provided the ability to express what I really felt inside. That is, my inner response to what was going on around me.

For example, when I wrote the original lyrics to my best known composition "He's Gonna Step On You Again", I was in South Africa during the apartheid era and the injustice of this regime caused me to look inside and ask myself how I really felt about the situation. At first it was merely an observation but as I looked deeper I started to react. This reaction led to the first line of the lyric... *"Hey rainmaker come away from that man, you know he's gonna take away your promised land."* Implying that what had happened to the Red Indians in North America was about to happen to the indigenous people of Southern Africa. This thought was then taken and expanded upon when I sat down with my song writing partner John Kongos, who shared the same views, and we completed the song.

Your attitude can change your behaviour

The world inside you is driven by your thoughts and your free will. By looking at the world "inside" – you will be challenged to examine your attitudes and values. Attitudes drive behaviour. Believe it or not, one of the best ways to change your behaviour is to change your attitude toward the object or situation in question. So, having a good attitude can change your behaviour and help you interpret life's experiences in such a way that you feel happy and optimistic rather than angry and frustrated. However, for you to remain "up" (and keep this positive mind set), your will is involved. You can decide for yourself whether to react in such a way that your responses are constructive and effective, or you can decide to react negatively, resulting in your responses being non constructive and ineffective. The decision is entirely yours!

In the height of my success in the music industry, I was always anxious about the future. Could I sustain my success? Was the next release going to be as good as the last one? This negative attitude did nothing but hold me back from reaching my full potential. We should never fear the future. We all embark on a lifetime of learning and growing – a lifetime of change. In this respect, we have little choice about it. Whether we are nurtured or not, guided or not, loved or not, we grow and we learn. We change and endure change, and this matter of change has considerable psychological impact. To the fearful change is threatening because it means that things may get worse. To the hopeful it is encouraging because it may cause things to get better. To the confident it is inspiring because it offers a challenge to make things better. Your character and frame of mind will determine how readily you choose change and how you react to any change that's imposed on you. Therefore, it is necessary to prepare yourself so that your mind remains open to change, and especially change that moves you closer and closer toward your goals.

Success has nothing to do with luck

Success isn't an accident, it's an ongoing decision making process involving a sequence of positive and constructive choices. In your life, you have probably had experiences where you've been unsure of what to do or in what direction to go. You have likely gone back and forth and felt more and more hesitant, uncomfortable and distracted. But then, you finally resolve your dilemma by making a clear decision – you choose one way or another. In looking back, you find that your decision or choice (at the time) was the turning point for you. Success emerged out of the direct decision or specific choice you made. I can recollect times in my life when this has happened and I consider those moments precious because they paved the way for significant achievements.

One such case was when our band had split up and I needed to either join another band or find something else to do. I chose change and answered an advertisement in Melody Maker for a production assistant. I was interviewed and got the job. The company Gem Productions was headed up by Laurence Meyers and Tony Defries and it was a hit-making machine. Every week one of their writers, artists or producers would have something in the charts. Tony Defries, who had mentored me, eventually took David Bowie and broke away to form Mainman. I went with him for a while but ended up being managed by Barry Krost who also managed Cat Stevens. The result being, I started working with Cat Stevens. These successes emerged out one decision I made!

As you read this book and explore the various avenues sign-posted, you will get in touch with your inner self and discover how to act more decisively. To many people this may sound like a daunting task, however, it is possible for you to become more expectant, disciplined, determined, optimistic, flexible, well-prepared and persistent. And as a result, when it is needed most, you will be able to make the right choices and enjoy life to the full. It's your life, it's your choice!

"Success is not to be pursued, it is to be attracted by the person you become."

Jim Rohn

PART ONE

The Law of Constructive Choice

It's Your Life, It's Your Choice

21

The Law of Constructive Choice

"One's philosophy is not best expressed in words; it is expressed in the choices one makes... In the long run, we shape our lives, and we shape ourselves. The process never ends until we die. And the choices we make are ultimately our own responsibility."

Eleanor Roosevelt

Looking ahead, there are certain attributes you will need to develop, or attitudes you will need to adopt, in order to be able to make "right" choices. However, you may also need to identify and understand the underlying laws that govern and shape success.

Over the years, I have studied numerous universal laws or principles and familiarised myself with the various components that make it possible for these laws or principles to work effectively.

For instance, in the fundamental Law of Sowing and Reaping (which is also known as the Law of Cause and Effect), discipline and expectancy must be present (operative) for the law to work in the positive. In order to reap a harvest you must become disciplined in your sowing and expectant for a significant return.

This may seem very simplistic, but it's the same with all universal laws. They are like the natural law of gravity, you can't see it, touch it or smell it, but jump off a building and it works every time.

Therefore, when using any universal law or principle you must know and understand which component parts should be present or active within that law, and then set in motion each component part to achieve your aims and objectives. Having knowledge of these laws and principles, and understanding how their integral parts empower them, takes everything out of the realm of chance and into the sphere of reality. Success then becomes systematic and far more predictable. Knowing these laws is like having a specific number you can dial, and each time you dial that number you expect to make the same connection. Every time! Taking this approach will steer you away from the harmful influences of the mysterious, the superstitious and the irrational. Your success is not down to luck! Instead, it's the practical application of tried and tested principles that will work every time you apply them correctly.

Within the Law of Constructive Choice, there are seven component parts that should be active for success to follow. As you study and learn to apply these 'power tools', you'll begin to understand how they all compliment each other. And when laid out correctly, they become a tapestry of personal character traits that are invaluable when having to make key decisions in life. However, each one should be accepted and embraced fully, and this requires thought and contemplation. They must all become well entrenched in your mental processes until they are habitual. The most important principle of personal success is simply this: *"You become what you think about most of the time."*

Even though many things we choose are directly linked to our personal needs, deep desires and hopeful expectations, the ability to make correct life choices can still be attained and employed correctly. In this regard, the way you choose to explain things to yourself is very relevant.

When you choose to see things a certain way, you will see only what you want to see. As a result, your decisions are affected by what you've chosen to see, and what you've chosen to see will determine who you are and what you eventually become. Perception is everything!

Your thoughts and feelings are continually changing and they are quickly influenced by the events around you. For example, when you receive a piece of good news, your attitude immediately brightens and you feel more positive toward everyone and everything. If, on the other hand, you unexpectedly receive some bad news, you can immediately become upset, angry, or frustrated – even if the news is inaccurate or untrue. So, it's the way you choose to interpret the event (to yourself) that ultimately determines how you react, and in turn, what decisions you make.

Your mind is like the transmission of a car. You have a forward gear, and you have a reverse gear. Only you can choose which direction to go. Yet, it does not take any more effort to go forward than it does to go backward. It's all in the decision making process. Similarly, you determine, by your own choices, which direction your life is going to go. When you decide which way you want your life to go, your thoughts will come in line with it. The day you make a positive decision about your life is the very day your world may change for the better. Every time you choose change, you engage your life into forward motion.

In the Bible there is an interesting passage where God calls the whole universe to be legal witness to a very powerful declaration He makes... *"This day I call heaven and earth as witnesses against you that I have set before you life and death, blessings and curses. Now choose life, so that you and your children may live."* This divine statement illustrates the absolute necessity for all of us to make the right choices. Choosing correctly can bring about prosperity in every area – mentally, emotionally, physically, materially and spiritually. But notice, these "life" choices also have the power to influence future generations. Now, that's something to seriously think about!

Accepting that productive and beneficial choices stem directly from a positive temperament, one that has been established through correct knowledge of self, is where you start. From there on, you need to adopt character traits (or attitudes) that will encourage a positive temperament. These include being:

Decisive - Expectant - Honest - Disciplined - Flexible - Wise - Persistent

If you are going to make "right" choices (by applying The Law of Constructive Choice), the seven attitudes or component parts listed above must be established – become personal qualities that are visible in your life. Let us now go through them in detail. You must learn to ...

Be Decisive

"The best day of your life is the one on which you decide your life is your own. No apologies or excuses. No one to lean on, rely on, or blame. The gift is yours – it is an amazing journey – and you alone are responsible for the quality of it. This is the day your life really begins."

Bob Moawad.

Every great leap forward in life is preceded by a clear decision, and decisive commitment to action. The ability to make good decisions is one of the most important skills you can possess. If you desire ongoing success you must develop the ability to make good or sound decisions. Without this ability you are a non-starter. All high-achievers are decisive in their thinking and in their actions. They think things through carefully and in advance. Rash decisions are never good decisions. You must decide what you want and then make definite decisions. After that, you must take specific actions to turn your decisions into realities, and this takes commitment.

Decision making is said to be a mental action or process leading to the selection of a course of action among variations.

Every decision making process produces a final choice. It can be an action or an opinion, and it usually begins when you need to do something but you do not know what. Therefore, decision making is a reasoning process which can be rational or irrational. Although you can never "see" a decision being made, you can presume from observable behaviour that a decision has been made. Decision making is a mental activity that connects commitment to action. Common everyday examples include; deciding what to eat and when to sleep or get up in the morning. In your personal life you may use one of many decision making techniques. These include:

- listing the advantages and disadvantages of each option you've identified,

- lipping a coin, cutting a deck of playing cards, or any other random and foolish method,

- accepting the first option that looks like it might achieve the desired result,

- prayer, revelation, or other forms of faith and prediction,

- concurring with a person in authority or an "expert,"

- calculating the value of each option available.

Commit to action

Whatever technique you end up using the result should always be the same – a commitment to action. After having acquired the degree or measure of knowledge you believe necessary for that specific situation, you must become fully committed to an action. But a word of caution, recent findings in neuroscience's have shown that, in decision making, your emotions usually play a larger role than acquired knowledge. So try not to make decisions based on how you are feeling. This way you will give yourself a better chance of making the right choices in life. When you have mastered your emotions you will be able to roll with the changes.

People who know how to control their feelings always act decisively. Therefore, you must decide exactly what you want and then make the right choices to turn it into reality, but without emotional attachment.

Along with being an entrepreneur, I am also senior pastor of a large church. As a leader who is constantly dealing with issues that seriously impact on peoples lives, I have disciplined myself not to listen to my feelings when making decisions. Fortunately, the Bible provides clear and concise information regarding personal conduct and responsibilities in all matters of life. Even when praying we are never encouraged to rely on our feelings. In fact, feelings only serve to hinder our faith. In business, becoming emotional is a recipe for disaster. There is a big difference between passion and emotionalism. Being passionate about something can home you in and assist you in the decision making process. However, every time you become emotional you hinder your ability to see clearly, and discern correctly, and are therefore never able to act decisively. Clarity produces decisiveness!

Develop the habit of decisiveness

Developing the habit of decisiveness can be the critical factor that enables you to take command of every situation, and in turn, secure your future. A decisive person is one who exercises good judgement by making sound and well-informed decisions. Being decisive also means making effective and timely choices. Decisiveness is understanding and recognising the full implications of your choices, and it is always proactive and achievement oriented. Decision making is something you should respect and desire to use effectively throughout your life.

Decisiveness is often defined as being *"characterised by firmness and selection."* Being decisive means that you have the ability to decide, and the strength to be fully committed to your decision. From the fortitude of a decision you then have the ability to act. Success always involves you being able to make key decisions effectively.

Decisiveness then simply means being in control of your own life. Decisiveness is both a skill you can build and an internal state you can summon when you need it. Decisiveness does not mean being stubborn, arrogant or hasty. Decisiveness is simply the ability to decide with speed and clarity. In any situation the ability to decide is crucial. Whether you are an emergency room doctor or a high school graduate debating what to do with your life, without clear decisions there can be no action and no results. Inside your head sits the most powerful processing unit in the known universe, but without 'decision' it goes unused.

Often the reason people aren't decisive isn't because they don't have an effective strategy for problem solving. Indecisive people act that way simply because they assume others will make better decisions for them. These people end up being subjected to the whims of others and have to rely on the thinking power of those around them to survive. What a sad state of affairs! Decisiveness means being able to make clear decisions on your own – quickly. Until you have made a clear decision for yourself, you are simply procrastinating and wasting time, and you will never have the quality of life you deserve.

Get as much information as you can

Being decisive is simply the most rational way to take on any problem. You observe the information you have available and then you decide what would be the most successful course of action. If it is possible to get more information, you must decide how and when to get it. If you can't get more data, you simply decide with the facts available to you. Instead of being decisive, most people use delaying tactics. They won't spend more time researching, so they simply avoid the decision entirely.

Asking someone who is dissatisfied with his life what he plans to do about it, he will usually respond in a confused way. Without a clear decision no progress can be made. Although it would be nice if we lived in a world where perfect and concise information can be retrieved instantly, being decisive ultimately means recognising when you already have the best information you are going to get. At this point you simply need to make a decision with the information at hand and quickly move on. Waiting any longer is just delaying the inevitable, so you must decide even in the face of uncertainty.

The best decision is the best one you can make with the information available at the time. Certainty doesn't exist in the natural world and only a fool will expect to find it. And anyway, the majority of decisions you face will not necessarily have huge repercussions for any mistakes. Often you will face greater consequences by making no decision at all than by making a bad one. Even if the decision was poor, that was simply the sacrifice necessary to gather more information and make a better decision next time. Remember this, not every decision you make will be right, however, you can make every decision right! A decisive person will learn from each decision made so that the next one is more likely to be correct.

Ultimately, decisiveness should produce a definite, accurate and reliable result.

Decisiveness as a Skill

The ability to make firm decisions quickly is a skill that can be practised. You can start by simply timing how long it takes you to make decisions. Minor decisions, such as what movie to see or restaurant to go to, should be made in thirty seconds to a minute. Major decisions should be made in less than five, even if that decision is to acquire more information so that a decision of action can be made more effectively. The next time you are deciding what to eat, time yourself and only give a minute to answer. Once you get used to making decisions rapidly you will start to realise that clear, firm decision making often results in better decisions – better than the ones where you process the same information over and over again. Running around in circles, is usually procrastination and not really problem solving.

Decisiveness as an Emotion

In light of what was mentioned earlier, this may sound like a contradiction. However, decisiveness is more than just a skill, it is sometimes a distinct feeling. There must have been moments when you felt decisive. Certainly it felt different than when you were confused and unsure. Decisiveness is similar to a feeling of confidence, strength or assuredness. Think back to a time when you felt particularly decisive. How did you conduct yourself in that state. The chances are; you stood tall, your movements were controlled, and your voice projected well. This physiology is critical to your feeling of decisiveness. When you are being indecisive, try stepping into that state and you will probably feel more able to make firm decisions.

Whether you desire to be a skilful decision-maker or not. Don't ever look for certainty in the world around you before deciding to act. This approach to life will limit your ability make progress. And don't wait for others to make decisions for you. Operate from an internal source of strength and decide on the right course of action. Be purposeful and choose for yourself. Every time you make a confident decision you place a stake in the ground, a point from which you can measure progress, fulfilment and accomplishment. Life's journey needs to be measured correctly if you are to judge yourself and your achievements accurately and honestly.

"Decisiveness is a characteristic of high-performing men and women. Almost any decision is better than no decision at all."

Brian Tracy – American Speaker, Author

Be Expectant

"Creative power is that receptive attitude of expectancy."

Thomas Troward

The world around us is permeated with expectations. Each individual's expectations will have a profound effect, not only on themselves, but also on the people around them. What you confidently expect, from both people and situations, will determine your attitude toward them more than any other factor. Expectations have the power to produce of their own kind. This is known as the 'Law of Genesis' or the 'Law of Expectations'. Essentially, good expectations produce good results and bad expectations bring about bad results. It's the intrinsic character of their source that determines the outcome. Therefore, whatever you expect with confidence becomes your own self-fulfilling prophecy. This also works in the negative. If you expect negative things to happen, you are usually not disappointed. What you confidently expect acts like a mirror in your life, whether positive or negative.

By being expectant you set yourself up to receive exactly what you are expecting. This is a very powerful principle because it can help you to make right choices even when you don't have every detail or resource available. As you predict likely outcomes, you create real expectations about future events. Then these future events will appear feasible and attractive. And you will know exactly how to get there by anticipating that you can, and will, 'make the right decisions'. This approach motivates you to act positively so that you make this "expected" future become a reality.

"...You see, really and truly, apart from the things anyone can pick up (the dressing and the proper way of speaking, and so on), the difference between a lady and a flower girl is not how she behaves, but how she's treated. I shall always be a flower girl to Professor Higgins, because he always treats me as a flower girl, and always will; but I know I can be a lady to you, because you always treat me as a lady, and always will." With this inspiring quotation from George Bernard Shaw's play, PYGMALION, Robert Rosenthal and Lenore Jacobson concluded their 1968 publication, PYGMALION IN THE CLASSROOM. Just as the character, Eliza Doolittle, suggests that a person's place in society is largely a matter of how he or she is treated by others, the Rosenthal / Jacobson study concluded that students' intellectual development is largely a response to what teachers expect and how those expectations are communicated.

The original Pygmalion study involved giving teachers false information about the learning potential of certain students in grades one through six in a San Francisco elementary school. Teachers were told that these students had been tested and found to be on the brink of a period of rapid intellectual growth; in reality, the students had been selected at random. At the end of the experimental period, some of the targeted students – and particularly those in grades one and two – exhibited performance on IQ tests which was superior to the scores of other students of similar ability and superior to what would have been expected of the target students with no intervention.

Self-fulfilling prophecy

These results led the researchers to claim that the inflated expectations teachers held for the target students (and, presumably, the teacher behaviours that accompanied those high expectations) actually caused the students to experience accelerated intellectual growth. Whether you are inclined to accept or doubt the findings of the Pygmalion study and other research supporting "self-fulfilling prophecy" effects, it seems clear that the power of expectations can affect life's outcomes in one way or another.

In your own personal life any genuine expectations concerning your loved ones, friends, colleagues and even your own future all tend to come true. Confident expectations exert a powerful influence on people and future events, for good or for ill. So you need to be very cautious with regards to the direction your expectations are being guided. If you want your expectations to be positive and effectual, you must first be sure they are headed in the right direction.

Here are three practical suggestions:

1. Always expect the best. Always assume the very best will happen, and remind yourself not to overreact if things do go wrong. Think exceptional thoughts and envisage the best results from the fruit of your labour. Then remind yourself, the only limitations are those you place on your own imagination!

2. Expect the best from those around you. Tell your family and friends that you truly believe in them; that you think they are wonderful; and that you love them dearly. But most of all, constantly tell them you are very proud of them. Praise raises expectations with both parties. Finally, assume the best will come out of every relationship, both at home and in the workplace, and I assure you that you will not be disappointed.

3. Expect the very best of yourself. See yourself as being a great achiever. Imagine that you have unlimited potential and that you are equipped with great abilities. Start believing that you can accomplish anything

that you put your mind to. Imagine that your future is limited only by the size of the vision you have for your life. Assume that your greatest moments lie ahead and accept that everything which has happened to you up to now has merely been preparation for greater things that are yet to come. Expect to succeed in all you put your hand to – nothing succeeds like success!

"Expectancy is the atmosphere for miracles."

Edwin Louis Cole – American Author

If we were to pursue this thought, that is, *"expectancy creates an environment where miracles are performed,"* then expectancy and faith must have much in common. The Bible tells us that faith is the substance of things hoped for – confidently expected. Consequently, that which you confidently expect is birthed through childlike faith. This principle has always fascinated me and is the central theme of my first book "What Matters Most." There is a direct correlation between expectancy, hope and faith. However, if faith is reliant on hope – confident expectation – then hope must be reliant on optimism. For, to be optimistic is to be full of hope! Therefore, your expectancy cannot be fully effective without a good measure of optimism mixed in.

Optimism forms a core part of your emotional life

If you wish to enjoy life to the full, you will have to root out self-defeating pessimism and replace it with an intelligent form of optimism. You can only expand the vitality and energy in your life when you understand what optimism really is, why pessimism smothers you, and why certain kinds of attitudes hold you back.

Optimism is an active, empowering, constructive attitude that creates conditions for success by focusing and acting on encouraging possibilities and opportunities. Optimism is the vital ingredient for a life that is creative, productive and enjoyable.

Research shows that optimists live longer, enjoy better health, and do better in relationships, work and play. For some, optimism comes naturally. For most, it is a positive attitude towards life that must be learned and cultivated. An optimistic person stands a better chance of making the right choice purely because he is always looking at the "up side." On the other hand, pessimistic people are always focused on the negative and their choices in life are affected by this negative view. I see both as people who are standing on top of the same mountain, the only difference is the view they've chosen to look at.

Optimism is the breeding ground for the miraculous

Optimism inspires and empowers people to believe that they can do more and be better than they ever have before. It's a strong and very powerful quality in your personal and professional life. Optimism is the foundation of a positive mental attitude. Optimism is the ability to find something worthwhile in every situation. It has been best defined as *"a generally positive and constructive response to stress or negative circumstances."* Optimists are *"Can do"* people. And if something goes wrong they simply say, *"Everything is going to work out for my good."*

Optimists focus on the future and not on the past. They look for an opportunity in every difficulty. Adversity is seen as an opportunity to excel. They think on what can be done now rather than focusing on what has happened in the past (or who is to blame for it). Above all optimists are determined enough to be solution oriented rather than problem focused. They pay more attention to finding the solution, to determining the next step, rather than sticking with the problem. Optimists believe that every problem merely creates an opportunity to effect positive change.

Optimism includes the assumption *"I can do something to change this situation for the better."* Defeatism or pessimism includes the assumption *"There's probably nothing I do that will make any difference."* Of course, when you're optimistic, you are more willing to take action to change things for the better, which increases the likelihood that things will change for the better. That's how optimism becomes self-fulfilling. But pessimism can also become a self-fulfilling prophesy. If there is some area of your life that you have decided you cannot improve, you will no longer try, which makes it more likely that it will stay the way it is (or even get worse).

Optimism is not the same as thinking positively, in fact, it is easier than thinking positively. It has far more evidence from scientific experiments proving its effectiveness than positive thinking does. More than thirty years of research and over 500 scientific studies have shown that what you say to yourself when you experience stress and adversity – your explanatory style – influences your performance, your mood, and even your health.

One of the first studies on the role of pessimism in causing illness was carried out at Virginia Tech in the mid-1980s. The study, following 150 students, found that the optimists had only half as many infectious illnesses and visits to the doctor than the pessimists. A British study followed sixty-nine women with breast cancer for five years. Those who optimistically fought the cancer were less likely to suffer a recurrence and more likely to survive than those who responded to their diagnosis with fatalistic passivity. The rare individuals who had survived after two bouts of cancer were those with an optimistic view of life. Therefore, not only does an optimistic attitude make you more likely to succeed, it promotes good health.

Optimism promotes good health

Optimism benefits health in four ways:

First, by replacing a sense of helplessness with a feeling of control, optimism boosts the immune system. This was clearly demonstrated in rat experiments performed by Madelon Visintainer. The rats who experienced "helplessness" through the experimental set-up were more vulnerable to tumour growth than those who were able to shut off the electric shocks they were given. Scientists believe this to be the same with people. Those who feel they have no control over their lives are more likely to get cancer than those who are in control.

Second, optimists will seek medical advice and stick to health programs better than pessimists. The pessimists, tell themselves *"...it doesn't matter what I do."* So they give up easily and fail to seek information and professional advice. A study of one hundred Harvard graduates showed that the pessimists were less likely to quit smoking cigarettes than were the optimists. Again, proving that optimists have greater control over their lives.

Third, the more negative experiences a person encounters, the more illness he will probably suffer. If, all in one month, you lose your job, break up with your spouse, and a friend dies, your chances of becoming ill increase considerably. Pessimists experience more of these negative events and emotions because that's where their lives are centred. Therefore, they take less action to prevent bad things happening, and when negative events do occur they make them seem worse by thinking negatively, and feeling helpless about them.

Fourth, research has shown that the company of others reduces stress and consequently boost the immune system. There is a clear correlation between resilience against illness and the degree of social support. Lonely people who have no close friends or who withdraw from social engagement when unhappy have a greater risk of illness. And when ill, such people are more likely to get worse. Most pessimists don't have any direction in life. They always appear lost and they take less action to seek support. Optimism wipes away passivity (the pity-party attitude), leading us to seek out other people's help. The company of others helps to reduce stress, thereby boosting the immune system.

This is why church life has proved so beneficial to many people around the world. Others, that are part of the same community, can help take care of us and encourage us to rest and keep focus when times are tough.

Unsubstantiated and exaggerated claims for the 'power of the mind' to influence the body are easy to find. Yet, the evidence now strongly suggests that the way we think and feel does in fact influence our lives (holistically) to a significant degree. A proverb says, *"As a man thinks, so he is."* This should not be terribly surprising! Not only does optimism feel good, not only does it make us more successful, it can also extended our lives by keeping us in optimal health. A good enough reason to be optimistic – don't you think?

I am the eternal optimist. Therefore, it is far easier for me to encourage people and motivate them into action. Our church recently bought a new building and at times the negotiations with the vendor turned into a dog fight. We had waited a very long time to find the right building and it had taken over two years for the purchase to be completed. During this period, everyone's expectations were high but they were not necessarily confident of the outcome. I had to regularly address the congregation in order to give an update and this is when my optimism paid off. Inside, I had a confident expectation of the outcome.

No matter what we were going through, and at times it looked like the negotiations had broken down, I was able to say with absolute assurance that the building is ours. My optimism, expressing itself through a confident expectation of the outcome, helped to keep everyone excited until we got the desired result. This was exactly what I was expecting!

Tips on how to become more of an optimist

1. The key to optimism is to maximise your successes and minimise your failures. Start by clearly identifying your successes and accomplishments.

2. It's good to look honestly at your shortcomings so you can work on them, but focusing on your strengths is far more beneficial.

3. Keep in mind that the more you practice challenging your negatives thought patterns, the more automatic it'll become. Don't expect major changes in thinking right away, but do expect them to become ingrained over time.

4. Understand that the past does not equal the future. Just because you've experienced pain or disappointment in the past does not guarantee that it's all going to happen again in the future.

5. Always remember that virtually any failure can be a learning experience, and an important step toward your next success.

6. Stop thinking about what is happening to you and start thinking about what you can make happen.

7. Look for the source of your pessimism. The sooner you can attribute your pessimism to a unique set of circumstances rather than the state of the world itself, the easier it'll be to change your perspective.

8. Be thankful. Make a list of the good things that have happened to you. The key to being an optimist is recognising the benefits and possibilities of any situation, and understanding that it could always be worse.

9. When you feel pessimism clouding your judgement, remind yourself that every minute counts, and any time spent agonising guarantees nothing but less time to enjoy whatever life might have to offer.

10. Smile. Studies have shown that putting a positive expression on your face can actually make you feel happier and more optimistic about the future.

"For myself, I am an optimist – it does not seem to be much use being anything else."

Sir Winston Churchill

Be Honest

"Whoever gives an honest answer kisses the lips."

Proverb 24:26

Honesty is a form of intimacy, and intimacy is necessary if your personal relationships are going to prosper. Making right choices out of established relationships is much easier and far more reliable. However, you can't establish a sound relationship with anyone unless you know yourself well enough to be transparent. Being honest with yourself, and with others concerning yourself, is necessary if you are to make the right choices in life. Self-awareness is a valuable asset when dealing with those ever-changing challenges confronting you – which makes sense when one considers that Greek philosophers gave the advice to "know yourself" thousands of years ago. Self-awareness means having a deep understanding of your strengths, weaknesses, emotions, physical needs, motives and motivations. People with strong self-awareness are neither overtly critical nor unrealistically optimistic. Rather, they are honest and transparent about themselves.

Assess yourself honestly

When you have developed a high degree of self-awareness you will be able to recognise exactly how your feelings affect you, other people, and your decision making process. Consequently, when choices need to be made, they are made with the full understanding of your strengths, weaknesses, needs and drives. If you can keep your emotions in check, they will cease to hinder beneficial change. People who assess themselves honestly – that is, self-aware people – are well suited to making the right choices at the right time.

But how can one recognise self-awareness? First and foremost, it shows itself as an ability to assess oneself realistically. People with high self-awareness are able to speak openly and accurately about their emotions and the impact they are having on their lives. Self-aware people can also be recognised by their self-confidence. They have a firm grasp of their capabilities and are less likely to set themselves up to fail. This means, not over-stretching or overextending when implementing any of their plans or actions. They also know, and have no problem with, asking for help. What's more, they prefer not to take on challenges that they know they cannot handle alone. In other words, they play to their strengths. I am a firm believer that we should strengthen our strengths and manage around our weaknesses.

Self-awareness extends also to a person's understanding of his or her values and beliefs. Someone who is highly self-aware knows where he is headed and why, so he will be able to avoid temptations that do not agree with his value system or beliefs. On the other hand, a person who lacks self-awareness is apt to make decisions that bring on inner turmoil and confusion by treading on buried values. The decisions and choices of self-aware people are fully integrated with their values and beliefs, and as a result, they find life more enjoyable. Self-aware people learn to appreciate "the moment." They are also self-motivated and generally quite enthusiastic.

Key Areas for Self-Awareness

Realistically, we are all complex and diverse. So to become more self-aware, we should develop an understanding of ourselves in many areas. Key areas for self-awareness include our beliefs, motives, personality traits, personal values, habits, emotions, and the psychological needs that drive our behaviours.

Personality. We don't normally change our personalities, values and needs based on what we learn about ourselves. But, an understanding of our personalities can help us find situations in which we will thrive, and help us avoid situations in which we will experience too much stress. For instance, if you are a highly introverted person, you are likely to experience more stress in a public or communal environment than a highly extroverted person would. So, if you are highly introverted, you should find situations and activities that are more compatible with your personality. Awareness of your personality helps you analyse such a decision.

Values and beliefs. It's important that we each know and focus on our personal values. For instance, if your first priority is *"being there for your children"* or *"your relationship with God,"* it's very easy to lose sight of those priorities on a day-to-day, moment-by-moment basis. During the workday, so many problems and opportunities may arise, and our lists of "things to do" can easily exceed the time we have to do them. Since few (if any) of those things pertain to what we value most, it's easy to spend too much time on lower priority activities. When we focus on our core values, we are more likely to accomplish what we consider most important. And, find enjoyment in what we are doing.

Habits. Our habits are the behaviours that we repeat routinely and often automatically. Ultimately, we don't really decide our future, we decide our habits – then, our habits decide our future. Although we would like to possess the habits that help us interact effectively with others, we can probably all identify at least one of our habits that decreases our effectiveness. To many of us, the bad habit of not listening or talking across other people's opinions hinders meaningful interaction and must be dealt with. All bad habits will eventually destroy relationships.

Needs. Many scholars have identified a variety of psychological needs that drive our behaviours such as needs for esteem, affection, belongingness, achievement, self-actualisation, power and control. One of the advantages of knowing which needs exert the strongest influence on our own behaviours is the ability to understand how they affect our interpersonal relationships. For instance, most of us have probably known people who have a high need for status. They're attracted to high status occupations, and they seek high status positions within their organisations. Such people also want the things that symbolise and authenticate their status. Your personal needs cause motivation; and when these needs aren't satisfied, they can cause frustration, conflict and stress.

Emotions. Understanding your own feelings, what activates them, and how they impact on your thoughts and actions is emotional self-awareness. If you were once excited about your job but are not excited now, can you get excited again? To answer that question, it helps to understand the internal processes associated with getting excited (in the first place). A person with high emotional self-awareness understands the internal process associated with emotional experiences and, therefore, has greater control over them. The best way to start is by looking on inside – at the world that triggers your emotions. Once you become familiar with this world and know how to control it, you gain ascendancy over all the negative feelings that cause you pain. What ever your mind cannot master it will eventually resent.

Emotional honesty means expressing your true feelings. To be able to be emotionally honest you must first be emotionally aware. This emotional awareness is related to your emotional intelligence. It is your emotional intelligence which gives you the ability to accurately identify your feelings.

Emotional intelligence may also give you the ability to decide when it is in your best interest to be emotionally honest by sharing your deep feelings with others. There are times however, when it is not healthy or safe for you to be emotionally honest. In general though, I believe we would be better off individually and as a society if we were more emotionally honest.

When we are more emotionally honest with ourselves we get to know our "true selves" on a deeper level. This helps us become more self-accepting. It could also helps us make better decisions about how to spend our time and who to spend it with.

If you are emotionally honest with others, it may encourage you to be more emotionally honest with yourself. Resulting in a greater self-awareness and honesty with those you are in relationship with.

How Self-Awareness Makes You More Effective

Self-awareness is a great asset. It helps you to find situations in which you will be most effective, assists with intuitive decision making, and aids stress management and motivation of yourself and others.

Knowing your strengths and weaknesses. Self-awareness helps you exploit your strengths and cope with your weaknesses. For instance, if you are someone who is good at "seeing the big picture" that surrounds decisions, but not as good at focusing on the details, you might want to consult friends, colleagues or loved ones that are more detail-oriented before making major decisions. Co-operation between big-picture-oriented decision makers and detail-oriented decision makers can produce high quality decisions.

Motivation. It's very difficult to cope with poor results when you don't understand what causes them. When you don't know what behaviours to change to improve your performance, you just feel helpless. Self-awareness is empowering because it can reveal where the performance problems are and indicate what can be done to improve performance.

In addition, awareness of your spiritual, material or psychological needs can increase your motivation by helping you understand and seek out the rewards that you really desire. Things such as; a sense of personal accomplishment, additional responsibility, an opportunity to help others, a flexible work schedule, or greater earning potential.

Self-awareness means knowing your values, motives, personality, needs, habits, emotions, strengths, weaknesses, etc. With a sense of who you are and a vision of the person you want to become, a plan for professional or personal development can be created. Moreover, self-awareness allows you to motivate yourself and manage your life better. It also helps you with your intuitive decision making, and helps you to lead and motivate others more effectively. Being honest with yourself – being self-aware – is truly very useful.

"Our lives improve only when we take chances – and the first and most difficult risk we can take is to be honest with ourselves."

Walter Anderson – American Author

Be Disciplined

"No life ever grows great until it is focused, dedicated and disciplined."
Unknown Author

As mentioned previously, I spent my early years as a professional musician working with some very famous people. The lifestyle I embraced was totally undisciplined and most of the people I hung around with lacked self-control. And yes, all the stories you've heard about rock musicians are true. We lived life to the max – at any cost! However, we did have ambition and drive and that's probably what contributed most to our successes. Yet everything was very hit and miss – totally unpredictable. Unlike classical musicians who spend much of their time perfecting their craft, we would only practice to the degree that was necessary to play well as a group or recording artist. Most of us relied heavily on our natural gifting to see us through.

I still remember clearly how undisciplined I was in key areas of my life.

And at the same time, I am quite amazed that I was able to achieve as much as I did. It was only when I started to study the Bible that self-control began to be important to me. I realised that self-control was necessary if I was to sustain the things I had worked so hard to obtain. I was always able to get there, but never able to stay there. I was always able to make money, but was unable to hang onto it. My life was living feast to famine!

I know now that self-control is essential for success, comfort and a happier life. In order to change circumstances and events in your life, you must not only be prepared to change but you must be committed to positive change. People who think they can make millions or attract a dream relationship without the sincere desire to change themselves are bordering on self-deception. In my experience "change" is required to bring new and better things into your life. If you are happy and content with what you've got, then feel free to wallow in what you have already achieved. However, if you desire to have more then be prepared for significant change. And this requires self-control.

Self-control is crucial to your success

How many times have you got all fired up about something and then only to find that your enthusiasm has evaporated into the atmosphere? How many times have you made a firm decision, and really meant it, saying: "I'm going on a diet" – "I'm not going to eat cake or chocolate." Only to find that a few days (or even a few hours) later, you've given in to your own lack of self-control and have gone back to the comfortable routine you're used to. This happens to everyone and it's only because you haven't exercised your self-control enough.

Self-control can be defined as, the means of attempting to guide behaviour along a specific path to a directed aim or goal. Self-control is perceived in a few ways. One of which is philosophical and might be described as the exertion of a person's own will on their personal self – their behaviours, actions, thought processes. Much of this comes from the perception of self and the ability to set up boundaries for that self.

Self-control can be expanded into several different areas. In respect to willpower, it is centred in the ability of a person to exert their will over the inhibitions of their body or mind. Self-control, like an ongoing inner conversation, is what frees us from being prisoners of our own feelings. People engaged in such a conversation feel bad moods and emotional impulses just as everyone else does, however, they find ways to control them and even to channel them into useful modes of behaviour.

People who are in control of their feelings and impulses are able to create an environment of trust and fairness. Therefore, signs of emotional self regulation are not hard to miss. They include; a propensity for reflection and thoughtfulness; comfort with ambiguity and change; and integrity – the ability to say no to impulsive urges. Like self-awareness, self-regulation often does not get its just deserts. The Bible tells us to hold every thought captive and make obedient to Christ. There are spiritual rewards for self regulation – for saying no to temptations.

Self-control enhances your integrity

Self-control or self-regulation will also enhance your integrity, which is not only a personal virtue but also a sign of strong character. Many bad things that happen in life are a function of impulsive behaviour. Most people rarely plan to do bad things, instead, an opportunity presents itself, and people with low impulse control end up doing it. By contrast, consider someone who is scrupulously honest. When challenged with a negative impulse, he or she will choose to counteract it with a positive thought or action – rising above temptation. To some people this may sound like some religious exercise, but in fact it's practical, sensible and essential to good human behaviour.

The first step in learning self-control or self-regulation is to realise that it is your own body and your mind that you are dealing with – no one else's! You can, and will, control them as soon as you choose to. Self control is something you must pursue in a determined and positive way if your are to achieve any of your aims.

Loosing self control leads to a life of poverty, stress, bad habits (of many kinds) and other things that make life unbearable. When you learn to recognise your faults and then acknowledge the things you're very good at, you will learn how to control yourself in a much better and more effective way. After you have identified your weaknesses, you can guard yourself by steering clear of the traps already set for you.

The Law of Control

There is another aspect of control that's important to your well-being, and that is "being in control." This is sometimes referred to as the Law of Control, but from the outset I must make it clear that this law has nothing to do with controlling others. Nor has it to do with high-and-mighty authoritarian or dictatorial attitudes. But rather, the "feelings of control," or lack of it, that effects your everyday life. You feel good about yourself to the degree to which you feel that you are in control of your own life. The reverse of this law is that you feel negative about yourself to the degree to which you feel your are not in control of your own life, or that you are controlled by other people or circumstances. So many people have fallen into this trap and spend their lives miserable and discouraged. You can choose to be in control or be controlled, it's entirely up to you.

The psychological profession has long recognised the importance of feelings of control as a critical element in human personality and performance. Psychologists believe that feelings of control can greatly impact on your mental disposition and may be a contributing factor in many personality disorders. The term they use is "locus of control." The locus, or place, of control refers to where ever you feel the control is located (in any part of your life). If you feel that you personally make decisions that determine the direction of your life, you are considered to have an "internal locus control." But if you feel that your boss, your bills, your husband or wife, your childhood experiences, your health, or anything else controls you, or forces you to do or refrain from doing what you really want, you are considered to have an "external locus of control."

Remember this, the location of this place of control in your thinking is a critical element in determining your personal health and well-being. Every one of us needs to be honest and sincere about where our place of control is located.

Become inside-minded

The best location of your place of control should be inside of you. When you develop an internal focus of control (when you become "inside minded"), you will have a sense that you are behind the wheel of your own life. You will feel that you are steering toward your destiny and that your future is in your own hands. This position creates very low stress levels and guarantees higher performance in all areas. In this setting, you instantly become more relaxed – a real pleasure to be around!

On the other hand, if you have an "external" locus of control, and you feel that what you are doing is being dictated by other people and outside pressures, then your stress levels will climb significantly and your personal performance levels will drop dramatically. All who have studied this area of human behaviour, and there has been 25 years of research in this field, agree that a sense of control is absolutely essential for you to perform at your best and enjoy life to the full.

You must therefore establish an internal focus of control for you to live a happy and stress-free life. In you, right now, is the power to deal with all those things (or people) that are causing you the greatest amount of stress, anger or frustration. The things that you feel you have little or no control over can be brought under your control once more. No one should live under the tyranny of "outside" control. But the Law of Control requires you to first except the inevitable – to accept change! Change is inevitable. Not only that, it is unavoidable! It is an accelerating factor. It is unpredictable and discontinuous. And, it is affecting every area of your life – whether you like it or not!

Setting goals gives you more control

Change is also very frightening for most of us. There is a deep-rooted desire on the part of many people to avoid change of any kind, even positive change. This is why setting goals is so important. Goals allow you to be in control by setting the direction of change. Goals assure that change in your life is predominantly in the direction that you want to go (the predestined path that's been mapped out by you). Goals give you complete control over critical elements of your life. Goals also give you a greater sense of personal power and confidence.

Failing to plan or set goals will invite disaster. By failing to plan, you are planning to fail. No one actually plans deliberately to fail. No one decides (in advance) to live a life of underachievement and frustration. But by failing to decide exactly what you want, and plan accordingly, you end up living unconsciously and unintentionally by accident – out of control.

People who live this way tend to be very negative, pessimistic and helpless, and they feel as though they have little or no control over their lives. Such people always blame others for the situation they're in and continuously make excuses for their problems. They think they are victims of circumstances or that everything is down to luck and good fortune. They develop a victim's mentality which hinders progress in all areas of life. The wonderful thing about goals is that the very act of setting goals frees you from living out of control and places you squarely behind the steering wheel.

Goal setting puts you in charge of your life and makes you feel good about yourself. This is why goal setting is referred to as the "master skill" of success. It is the one skill that is probably more important to your overall happiness than any other skill you can develop. It puts you where you need to be – at the helm! You can take control of your life by: (a) Shifting to *"internal locus control,"* (b) controlling change through goal setting, (c) controlling your thought life.

Start by examining your life carefully and taking note of the parts of your life that cause you the greatest amounts of stress, anger, or frustration on a regular basis. You will find that these are usually situations in which you feel you have little or no control. The starting point of dealing with any stressful person or situation is for you to identify it clearly. Once you have identified areas of stress clearly, you must make a quality decision in each of these areas, to either get in or get out, to do something or stop something that you are doing. Whether it is a job, a relationship, or an emotion, the act of making a decision to take an action will reduce your stress. You will also increase your sense of personal power almost immediately.

Why not identify the areas in your life where you feel trapped, where you feel as if there is nothing you can do about it. Then ask yourself this, *"What one change can I make that will put me back in control?"* Whatever the answer, resolve to do something about it immediately. And remember, you are where you are and what you are because of yourself, because of your choices and your decisions. If you are not happy with a situation, it is up to you to make different and better choices or decisions. You are free to choose change. You are free to take control of your life. So just do it! You'll enjoy being in control. It's your mind, it's your body and it's your choice.

> *"You must admit you have self-control before you can use it."*
> Carrie Latet – Author / Poet

Self-control and preparation go hand-in-hand. A well disciplined person will always be well prepared. In life, there's simply no substitute for hard work – for doing one's homework and basically preparing for every challenge. No one ever topped an exam, cleared a crucial hurdle or excelled at a particular sport by taking it easy and being totally unprepared. Preparation will fill you with confidence and a winning spirit, and it will help you achieve the goals you've set out for yourself. Preparation also requires a lot of faith because you have no guarantee that your preparation will pay off. You simply have to believe, deep within yourself, that everything you do of a constructive nature will come back to you in some way.

You have to know that every good effort is never wasted. That what you sow, you will eventually reap. Therefore, you have to be willing to sow for a long time before you reap, knowing that if you do sow in quality and quantity, the reaping will definitely come about within the force of this law.

Preparation is the key

In everything you do, in everything you plan, preparation is the key. If you want to be ready for success, you have to plant the seeds of success well in advance of the harvest that you expect. Do what other successful people do: "Think on paper." The A scripture says, *"Write the vision down and make it plain to see, that you may be energised every time you read it."* And most of all, remember this: *"Everything counts..."* Everything you do is either moving you toward your goals or moving you away from them. Everything is either helping you or hurting you. Nothing is ever neutral. Everything does count! So write it down, and be prepared.

It's all very much in the detail. Once you have clarified your ideas and looked at all your options, it's time to starting putting some plans in place. Whatever you've chosen to do, making it happen takes time and preparation. Having a clear plan keeps you on track, allows you to see how much progress you've made and avoids wasting unnecessary time. *"Preparation is key to the success of any venture."* Effective performance is preceded by painstaking preparation.

The mark of any professional, in any field, is that he / she takes far more time to prepare than the average person. The non-serious (unprofessional) person always attempts to bluff or "wing it." He tries to get by with minimum preparation and little effort. But be careful here, your level of preparation is blatantly evident to everyone around you. When you're not prepared, you have nothing to hide behind.

Preparation requires faith but it calls for a good measure of self-discipline too. It demands self-discipline because our natural tendency is to do more and more of those things that come most easily to us, and to avoid those areas that we don't enjoy because we're not particularly good at them. It requires a strength of character that allows us to admit our weaknesses in a particular area, and then the resolve to go back to work in order to develop those weaknesses so that they don't hold us back. Therefore, in your preparation for success you must remember to be honest with yourself, especially when examining your strengths and weaknesses.

One of the greatest changes that has ever taken place in our society happened in 1989 when the world changed from the Industrial Age to the Information Age. We are now living in an information-based society. Because of the internet and other technological advances more than 60 percent of the working population is in the business of processing information in some way. This means that we are now living in a knowledge-based society and you have to be a person of knowledge if you're going to succeed. To succeed you must be able to work with your mind, your mental talents and abilities. Gone are the days of labouring in the factories and the mills. Today you can succeed only by clear and concise thinking, and the more effectively you think and the better prepared you are mentally, the more productive and positive you'll be.

As a young man Abraham Lincoln said this, *"I shall study and prepare myself and some day my chance will come."* If you study and prepare yourself, your chance will come as well. There is nothing you cannot accomplish if you'll invest the effort to get yourself ready for the success that you desire. And there is nothing that can stop you but your own lack of preparation. Abraham Lincoln recognised early on, as do all great men and women, that painstaking preparation was the key that could unlock his future. Great successes are more than often determined by attention to the smallest details. One inaccuracy can make all the difference. And everything does count!

So do your homework because inevitably it's the details that will trip you up. Someone once said, *"No one every gets bitten by an elephant, it's the mosquitoes every single time."* It's the little things that sting you and irritate your life.

Condition yourself to finding the facts

Condition yourself to seek and find the real facts – this is wisdom. Don't always go for the obvious ones, but on the other hand, avoid the obscure facts or the assumed facts. Get hold of the real, substantiated facts! Real facts don't lie. Even after been checked and double-checked, the real facts always reveal the same information. And constantly remind yourself that your thinking and your decisions are only as good as the quality of the information you have to work with. Taking action before getting the real facts, or thinking through all the details, is a recipe for disaster – it breeds mediocrity and brings about failure. The reverse of this action, of course, is that action preceded by accurate information, clear and concise thinking, and thorough planning, is the reason for virtually every success. This doesn't mean that you will automatically succeed if you plan thoroughly in advance. But it does mean that you will almost always fail if you don't! So don't assume anything or take anything for granted. If it's important enough to matter to you, then it's important enough to check and double-check.

In every activity you can get involved in, whether it be a skill, a sport or a profession, preparation is a vital key to your success. Therefore, take your time to think through your most important tasks and responsibilities. Then write them down. This way you can list every detail of the matter and review your notes carefully. And whenever necessary, get some advice. Try to obtain the thoughts and opinions of those you trust before you make a major decision or a serious commitment to anything. Look for someone who has been where you are and who has better skills than you at that particular moment in time. Ask yourself this, *"What insights can he or she give me?"*

We all need to keep learning in order to keep growing. Today, we live in a knowledge-based society, and knowledge in every field is doubling approximately every two to three years. This means that you must double your knowledge in your field every two to three years just to stay in touch. You've most likely already reached the ceiling in your career – using your current level of knowledge, talents and abilities. Therefore, if you want to go faster and farther, you must get back to work and begin to prepare yourself for greater things. To achieve this, you may need to turn off the television and politely excuse yourself from aimless socialising and get back to working on yourself. There's no better investment in life than the good things you deposit in yourself. Your possibilities are endless, your potential is unlimited, and your future will open up for you when you prepare yourself for the success that must inevitably be yours.

"So prepare for a chance of a lifetime. Be prepared for sensational news. A shining new era is tiptoeing nearer. And where do we feature? Just listen to teacher."

"Be Prepared" from the musical the Lion King by Elton John and Tim Rice

It's Your Life, It's Your Choice

Be Flexible

"I am a man of fixed and unbending principles, the first of which is to be flexible at all times."

Everett Dirksen

To be flexible in everyday life (and business) you need to 'go with the flow' – be adaptable. As a musician my genre was The Blues, and to be a good blues player you must be able to improvise. Good musical improvisation requires complete flexibility and adaptability. Without it there is no flow and no expression, and therefore, no "feel". I believe it's the same in whatever you do in life. You need to welcome change as a genuine opportunity, not a threat. As with the other character traits we've already examined, you must also keep a positive mental attitude.

The only things you can control in life are your responses to the inevitable problems and difficulties you may face each day. How you respond to any situation, or how you interpret the situation, then determines the clarity and effectiveness of your thoughts and your responses.

The more positive your thoughts are, the more creative you will be also. Consequently, you will be able to tap into a reservoir of new ideas that can help overcome every difficulty. And when it comes to life's problems, I assure you, will need to be creative and flexible (open to new ideas). Personal fulfilment is a creative exercise in achieving goals, accumulating ideas, and investing your time wisely. But it all hinges on how flexible you are prepared to be.

Flexibility is the mark of a superior mind

Many successful people believe that flexibility is probably the single most important quality you can develop in order to reach your goals in a fast-changing modern society. It is the mark of a superior mind – a superior attitude. When you set a clear goal or objective for yourself and make a plan, you usually have a fairly good idea of what it is you will have to do to get whatever it is you want to achieve. However, there are many things that can change, each of which may require changes to your initial plan. The most enthusiastic and creative people are those who are open and flexible in the face of the inevitable changes they are required to make as they move toward their goals.

Therefore, success is best achieved when you are clear about your goal but flexible about the process of getting there. So don't frustrate yourself by keeping to the same plan when it is obviously not working. If you are experiencing continued resistance and frustration, it's probably an indication that you are doing the wrong thing. Whenever you feel that you are trying too hard and getting too few results, be prepared to stand back and re-examine your affairs. And remember, never get emotionally attached to what you do. What you do and who you are is very different. I have met too many people who cannot be flexible simply because their identity is enveloped in what they do. As an entrepreneur I never get emotionally attached to any of the projects I'm involved in (which is usually four at any one time). But this wasn't always the case. I started off being very inflexible because every project was like a baby to me.

I couldn't let go of it, at any cost, and this often led to hardship and disaster. Now I've learnt to go with the flow. I have an idiot-proof approach, and that is, to simply follow the one that has legs! In other words, I follow the project that has traction – the one which is already in motion. This doesn't mean I've given up on the others, but it allows every project to incubate and grow at it's own pace, without me interfering with this natural process. And all the time I remain open to change.

Remain flexible and change your approach

Being able to remain flexible is not easy for most people. They like the comfort of 'predictability'. Therefore, I suggest that you first make sure the goal which you are pursuing is still the goal that you truly desire. Then seriously consider the possibility that your strategy may be the wrong one for the situation you are presently in. Be fully prepared to reconsider and change your approach. Especially, get your ego out of the way. Remain flexible in your decision making – be open to change. High achievers are not necessarily those who make the right decisions all the time, but they are those people who make their decisions right. They are quick to accept feedback and self-correct. They take in new information and are prepared to change if necessary. But they are always decisive, always moving forward, never wishy-washy in their attitudes and their approaches to life.

Therefore, whenever your plans don't seem to be bearing fruit, instead of pushing even harder, stop, re-evaluate the situation and change your approach. Opinionated, stubborn people are unable to be flexible, and therefore, unlikely to make the right choices. Consider the possibility that you could be wrong in your present course of action and the decisions you've made. Then, where necessary, cut off the dead wood and revise your plans until they enable you to move forward smoothly, without anxiety or frustration. Remember, crisis is often change trying to take place. So make room for change in the midst of every crisis.

When you experience a crisis or roadblock of any kind, stand back for a moment and ask your self, *"What change is trying to take place here? What is the message for me that's contained in this crisis?"*

You may be having a crisis in your work, in your personal relationships, or with your health. In almost every case, a crisis is a clear indication that something is definitely wrong and that pursuing the same course of action will only make it worse. So stop blaming everyone else for your problems. Rather, seek to discover, and then to understand, what positive change is trying to take place in your life right now. Be assured, you will get the answers. But you must ask, seek and then wait until you have a full understanding of the situation.

Never be presumptuous. Never assume that you have all the answers, and always remain open-minded. One definition of a fool is; someone who keeps doing the same thing and expects different results

Incorrect assumptions are fatal

Incorrect assumptions lie at the foot of every failure. Almost every failure you experience will be because of an incorrect assumption that you made, and then accepted. When things aren't going well it is very wise to question your assumptions. What are your assumptions? What if your most cherished assumptions were wrong? What changes would you have to make immediately to get things back on track? If you have achieved your goals it is probably because the assumptions you were operating on turned out to be consistent with the reality of the situation.

Whenever you experience setbacks and failure, it usually means that there is something wrong with your basic premises, your assumptions. Any inconsistency when it comes to discerning the reality of the situation will cause you hardship, and may bring about disaster. The Reality Principle states: you should always operate in the reality of every situation, and not on what you would like it to be or how you assume it to be.

Your willingness to test your assumptions against reality, combined with the willingness to accept the possibility that you may be wrong, is the attitude that will ultimately lead you to great achievement. But remember, this is not possible if you are rigid and set in your ways. So remain flexible!

How do you stretch your thinking and become more flexible?

Mental flexibility is an exercise. Flexing your mental abilities isn't that different than flexing your physical muscles. Here are some ways to stretch your mind – to make your thinking more flexible:

1. Listen to people that you disagree with. Take in their arguments and follow their logic. Try to see things entirely from their point of view and not your own. You'll be surprised at the outcome.

2. Stay with a global view. Don't get caught in semantics or in details. Words may not be your best friend when you're looking for flexibility. Words sometimes tie things down in a precise detailed fashion – a fashion that might be wrong. Therefore, in some circumstances words can even confuse rather than add clarity. So keep thinking "big picture" and remain flexible.

3. Give unconventional ideas a voice. Think out of the box and push past the normal parameters. Let other people have a chance to share their "off the wall" ideas. Maybe try them out! You might decide that you really like one.

4. Make a habit of questioning yourself. Why am I doing this? Is there another approach? Is this my own thinking or just a habit I'm used to? The hardest part is to remember to question yourself. Doing it is actually fun. Once you get into the habit, you'll not only gain flexibility, your productivity will also increase.

5. Find the humour and laugh more. Laughter is medicine. There is something funny about almost everything and every situation, provided you open yourself up to it. So give yourself reason to laugh, and you may find that other creative ideas come easier too.

6. Wake-up and dream. Rewrite reality and embrace a few impossibilities. Don't just dream – pull the lid off – blow your mind. Push your thinking in every direction you can. It doesn't hurt, and the investment pays off in your ability to think in a dimension where other people can't. Go where no man has gone before!

Mental flexibility might be the one skill that has the most visible impact in your life. Mental flexibility straightens the bend, unties the knot, and frees-up every bottleneck. Flexible thinking is a skill that all of us need to develop. Stop thinking about where you've been and start thinking about where you're going. The future is an exciting place! Every road you take during life's journey is crowded with undulations and bends. So remain flexible – and enjoy the thrill of it!

"Stay committed to your decisions, but stay flexible in your approach."

Tom Robbins – American Novelist

Be Wise

> *"Never mistake knowledge for wisdom. One helps you make a living, the other helps you make a life."*
>
> Sandra Carey

In the early 80's I remember comparing my new-found Christian values with those which were around when I was active in the music business. And I must say, it was quite an eye opener. After all, I was used to living in the fast lane – running on bald tyres!

So what was the main difference between the new and the old person (in the natural, not spiritually)? I still looked the same, had the same voice, and even had the same mannerisms. I felt that I needed to know the answer to this question, but didn't find it until one day I visited a large church in Tulsa, Oklahoma. It was my first trip to that part of the US and I had decided to go to an evening service just to see what it was like. There must have been 2000 people attending and the atmosphere was electrifying.

After the service had ended, this small man appeared out of the crowd and came running up to me, *"It's you, come here, I need to pray for you"*, he said. If he hadn't startled me I might have said something, but instead I let him go ahead and pray. These were his words, (I will never forget them)... *"Father God, I pray that you give this man a double portion of your wisdom."* Then he calmly walked away.

Now, this may not seem that strange to some of you. However, the week before, when I was at our church in South Africa, I had come out for prayer because I was feeling quite unwell at the time. There were at least thirty other people that had also come forward, and when the pastor eventually got to me he looked me in the eye and said this, *"I pray for a double portion of wisdom."* Notice, I had heard the very same phrase from two entirely different people, in two different countries... *"A double portion of wisdom."* This is when I finally realised what actually distinguishes me from my past. Before my conversion, I never had any wisdom – not one once of it! And my lifestyle had been a testimony to this. But the sad thing is I never wanted it either. There's a proverb that says, *"Wisdom is the principle thing, therefore, get wisdom. And in all your getting, get understanding."*

Wisdom is not mystical

Wisdom is something every one of us can acquire and apply to our lives effectively. But in order to do this we need to understand what wisdom is. There are many definitions of wisdom and also many views on how it can be acquired and how it should operate. Learned scholars have sought its revelation and ancient philosophers have provided many of its quotes. In fact, the word 'philosophy' means 'love of wisdom.' Philosophers say they love wisdom and they believe there are four general approaches to understanding what is wisdom: (1) wisdom as humility, (2) wisdom as accuracy, (3) wisdom as knowledge, and (4) wisdom as knowledge and action.

All of these approaches maintain that a wise person instinctively knows "what is important in life." However, views differ, for the most part, over what it is that the wise person must know and whether there is any action that is required for wisdom to manifest.

Aristotle distinguished between two different kinds of wisdom, theoretical wisdom and practical wisdom. Theoretical, or philosophical wisdom, is, according to Aristotle, "scientific knowledge, combined with intuitive reason, of the things that are highest by nature". For Aristotle, theoretical wisdom involves knowledge of necessary principles and the propositions that can be logically deduced from them. Aristotle's idea that scientific knowledge is knowledge of necessary truths and their logical consequences is not a widely accepted view. However, this classical view – theoretical wisdom and practical wisdom – does line up with the apostle Paul's understanding of wisdom.

In his writings, Paul used two separate Greek words when referring to wisdom. The one word "sophia" concerned having knowledge of (or insight into) the true state of affairs – how things really are. The second word "phronesis" referred to the application of such knowledge – what one does with it. Therefore, it is one thing to know how everything is placed (theoretical wisdom), but this knowledge has no value unless it is applied correctly (practical wisdom). Note, both Aristotle and Paul defined wisdom as simply putting acquired knowledge into practice.

Some people believe wisdom is knowing how to, and succeeding at, living well. But anyone who is attracted to the idea that knowing how to live well is a necessary condition for wisdom might want to consider cases in which a person knows all about living well, yet fails to put this knowledge into practice. Knowledge is always easier than action. Therefore, to acquire wisdom is to seek both the theoretical and the practical, and then to use them together correctly. This way you will have the wisdom to make the right choices or decisions and benefit from both knowledge and action.

Wisdom can't be taught

Experiential knowledge is greater than passive knowledge. Wisdom is a trait that can be developed by experience, but not taught. Concerning experience, C. S. Lewis said this, *"What I like about experience is that it is such an honest thing... You may have deceived yourself, but experience is not trying to deceive you."* Experience allows you to see things as they are! Edith Wharton said: *"Life is the only real counsellor; wisdom unfiltered through personal experience does not become a part of the moral tissue."* I am convinced that it is only after you have gained enough information, through personal experience, that you can acquire true knowledge – knowledge that's become a part of you. Likewise, it's only after you have built sufficient character through experiential knowledge, that you can operate effectively in wisdom. In a sense, knowledge shrinks as wisdom grows. The active and effective utilisation of well-understood principles (acquired through personal experience), is the final possession of wisdom.

If you understand that success, happiness and life-balance come from living in harmony with timeless principles, then you too can seek to discover the wisdom of the ages, and when you've found it, you can apply it to the challenges of today. Sophocles said, wisdom is the supreme part of happiness. By consciously making a decision to seek after and live by wisdom you place yourself on the path to success and true happiness. It also gives you the peace that only comes with being a seeker of wisdom and truth.

Experience enables you to make good choices

Of course, you don't have to experience everything in life to know what paths to avoid. You have a conscience and common sense to draw on. But it is experience – good or bad – that gives you the knowledge to make good choices.

It might be your experience with the grief of a difficult relationship or the joy of a strong one that causes you to value relationships. Or, it may be your experience with the anguish of bad debt or the satisfaction of accruing interest that causes you to value financial advice. But in each case, it's experience that helps you to know what is best for you and which path to take. This is referred to as navigational intelligence.

Francis Hutcheson, a Scottish philosopher said this, *"Wisdom denotes the pursuing of the best ends by the best means."* Top author Roger Merrill wrote, *"The more you learn to value principles, evaluate experience and invite inspiration, the stronger your navigational intelligence or "wisdom" will be."*

So how do you gain the most from experience? Well, you need to process your experiences correctly. You need to ponder over them, reflect on them, and gain insight and understanding from your encounters with the affairs of everyday life – good or bad. Your ability to evaluate and learn from your experiences is one of the best ways to move toward knowledge and understanding, and in turn, acquire wisdom. And in the act of acquiring wisdom you must gain understanding. And true understanding is only established after you have processed and evaluated your experiences correctly.

Two things you can do that will help you in this area:

Learn from the experiences of others. In addition to learning from your own experiences, you can choose to learn from the experiences of others. Choose to learn from other people's mistakes so that you can change for the better. Aristotle said, *"A wise man learns from a fool, but a fool can't learn from a wise man."* You can learn from any person who is willing to share his/her experiences openly. This way, you are invited into the hearts and minds of others, so the learning goes well beyond mere behaviour and into motive and profound meaning. One of the great benefits of rich relationships is shared learning.

Share your experiences with others. This leads us to another wisdom path; sharing what you have learned with others. By sharing in this way, you align your life with the principle of contribution. And your contribution toward others determines life's contribution toward you. In addition, you open meaningful dialogue that creates a bridge between your own experiences and the experiences of others. Then, as you interact, going back and forth across the bridge, you create a larger shared vision.

Understanding for both of you is increased, and you become wiser together – wiser than you could ever have become alone. This can be an extremely valuable connection between two people.

As mentioned, if the link between information and knowledge is experience; and the link between knowledge and wisdom is character. Then it's not enough to only "know" the principles that bring positive results, or know exactly "how" to do them; it's also the "doing" of them. And, doing them for the right reasons, at the right time, and in the right way. This is called insight, and insight, like wisdom, lets you see the way things really are. But such insight must be applied to be useful, and this is a practical every day routine.

Too many people get hooked on "knowing." Most of you probably "know" more than you need to know in almost every area of your life. This is why living with an awareness that processing your own experiences correctly is so vital. You can learn about universal principles – you can read about the experiences of others – but the place you really develop navigational intelligence (wisdom) is on the sea of life. That's where your learning becomes firsthand – up close and personal! That's where experiential knowledge, properly processed, becomes wisdom.

As you boldly confront the challenges of daily living, with poignant awareness, you learn to set your compass and chart your course based on "the truth" you have acquired firsthand.

Each day of your life is an unknown, unwritten page. No one has complete knowledge of the future (except God). However, if you value good principles, learn from your experiences, and then keep trying no matter what – you will acquire and exercise sufficient wisdom to live joyfully and successfully. It's your life – it's your choice!

"Wisdom is not a product of schooling, but of the lifelong attempt to acquire it."

Albert Einstein

It's Your Life, It's Your Choice

Be Persistent

"Persistent people begin their success where others end in failure."

Edward Eggleston

Persistence and failure cannot coexist. Failure happens when you quit. When all is said and done, persistence is the ultimate success insurance. Nothing can take its place. Being determined and persistent in life is very important. Something that's absolutely necessary if you are going to achieve your goals. We all love reading about the lives of people who faced adversity – yet succeeded by being persistent. Famous individuals who never quit and finally realised all their dreams. The courage they displayed was only matched by their persistence in the face of extreme challenges and impossibilities. But sometimes, rather than help us or spur us on, such wonderful examples serve only to make us feel more inadequate. Yet, such great accomplishments are never really about the amazing strength our heroes have exhibited, rather, it's about their strong 'desire' to succeed.

Persistence and desire are connected

Your persistence and determination is directly linked to your desire. You'll never leave where you are, until you desire to be somewhere else. Your degree of desire will determine how persistent you will become. If you want or need something bad enough, you will develop the mindset and energy level to persevere all the obstacles and disappointments put before you. All of us need to be positive and persistent as we face life's challenges. But at the same time, we must set an example and be a role model for those looking on, so they also won't quit when the going gets tough. If you are unwilling to loose, and make an extra attempt, rarely will you lose.

Persistent people diligently sort through obstacles and practice perseverance, while others merely execute their well thought out plans and objectives. This quality of persistence grows stronger as you recognises that it helps you to "get exactly where you want to go!" Once you have determined exactly what it is you want to accomplish, you need to take deliberate action on a consistent, persistent basis in order to succeed. Think of it like building a muscle. If you have never weight trained before, the first time you walk into a gym, chances are you will not be able to bench press 250lbs. However, if you are persistent, and you consistently go back to the gym, you will find yourself getting stronger and closer to your goal with each and every visit.

One of the things you'll notice on your journey towards your goals, are roadblocks. That is, you will encounter obstacles that seem to jump out of nowhere in an attempt to halt your progress. Accept these obstacles, as they are a part of life. If you were cushioned from every blow you'd never grow. Everyone would have every success they ever wanted if there were no obstacles. Your role is to be persistent and work through those obstacles. If you find little or no resistance along the way, chances are you are not really challenging yourself. And when you eventually reach your objective, you won't experience the feeling of 'sweet success'.

So make your goal a challenging one. If you can achieve it right now, with the abilities and resources you have, it's definitely not the right goal. There needs to be a little of the impossible present for it to be the right one.

Don't be afraid to fail

Failure is not terminal! If you take the time to study any successful person, you will learn that the vast majority of them have had more 'failures' than they have had successes. This is because successful people are very persistent; the more they stumble and fall, the more they get right back up and get going again.

On the other hand, people that don't get back up and try again, never attain any success. For example, Walt Disney was turned down 302 times before he got financing for his dream of creating the *"Happiest Place on Earth"*. Today, due to his persistence, millions of people have shared 'the joy of Disney'. Colonel Sanders spent two years driving across the United States looking for restaurants to buy his chicken recipe. He was turned down 1,009 times! How successful is Kentucky Fried Chicken today? Having said this, keep in mind that you must constantly re-evaluate your personal circumstances and the approach you are using to reach your desired goal.

There is no sense in being persistent at something that you are doing incorrectly! Sometimes you may have to modify your approach along the way. You may have to adjust your course or change your destination. But do whatever it takes, and decide to be persistent at any cost. Next time you deliberately move toward a goal, remind yourself that you can learn from your mistakes. This will help you to look for a better way of doing it without the fear of failure. Those individuals we use as examples of persistence in adverse conditions, never feared failure. They just kept on going, or made an extra effort when it mattered most. Does this qualify them for "genius" status? Probably not. They were simply not prepared to give up!

The main reason there's been so many failures among those who started out with high hopes, is that they lacked "staying" power. They could not stay the course: and what's the point in running if you can't do the distance? Persistence outlasts every battle. It's light is seen long after the dust has settled. Persistence never stops to consider whether it is succeeding or not. The only question is how to keep pushing ahead. How to get a little further along, a little nearer to the finishing post. Whether it means climbing mountains, crossing rivers or ravines, persistence has the resolve to get there. Every other consideration is sacrificed for this one dominant purpose. Genuine persistence is insistent on gaining ascendancy, and it is prepared to overcome every weakness – physical, mental or moral. Great success comes from great determination, great self-discipline and self-mastery. And I believe this is equal to genius itself!

Genius is often perseverance in disguise

No amount of genius ever had a significant effect on anything, except when being enforced with the "staying power" to overcome all obstacles that presented themselves. I admire a person who rises above the circumstances in which he was born, to become greater than his allotment in life. Tenacity of purpose never changes through the ups and downs, or if there's a sudden turn of events, it chooses to conquer all opposition in order to arrive at its chosen destination. Tenacity of purpose, perseverance, persistence, determination, and consistency of intention are all one. They set genius in motion! But genius left unexecuted is no more genius than an unlit lamp is a light to the room.

Today is the day to begin your new journey, using tenacity of purpose and consistency of intention, take a giant step towards tomorrow's successes. Stop looking at where you have been and start looking at where you can be. Stop thinking about what has happened, and start thinking about what you can make happen. The staying power is already in you – so aim to go the full distance. Be prepared to push everything over the line – no matter what!

Here is a list of people who were persistent and persevered despite handicaps and disabilities:

- Beethoven (composer) – was deaf
- Ray Charles (musician) – is blind
- Thomas Edison (inventor) – had a learning problem
- Albert Einstein (scientist) – had a learning disability
- Terry Fox (runner) – is an amputee with cancer
- Stevie Wonder (musician) – is blind
- James Earl Jones (actor) – was a stutterer
- Helen Keller (author) – was deaf and blind
- Marlee Matlin (actress) – is deaf
- Franklin D. Roosevelt (president) – was paralysed from polio
- Vincent Van Gogh (artist) – was mentally ill
- Woodrow Wilson (president) – had a learning problem
- Itzhak Perlman (concert violinist) – was paralysed from the waist down

A productive life is not an accident

"Patience, persistence and perspiration make an unbelievable combination for success."

Napoleon Hill – American Author

Patience, persistence and perspiration = resolve. A productive life is not an accident, and how far you go in life is not determined by external factors – by what's happening outside and around you. It is largely determined by internal factors, by what's going on inside. The world inside you ascertains the level of success you are able to achieve, and how far you are prepared to go. And this world is seriously influenced by desire. Therefore, how high you rise is mainly dependent on how high you want to climb. Your own personal level of desire may govern your achievements more than any other factor. The Greek word for desire (thelema) literally means, "to will," "to wish" or "that which is willed." It implies a strong determination. This being the case, any form of human accomplishment must involve desire – a resolve or determination to succeed.

Desire is one of the strongest emotions and one of the greatest forces inside of you. When harnessed properly it can give you everything you have ever wanted. Desire is the fuel for success. Just as a car or any other vehicle needs fuel to keep going, a man's desire is what drives him and it will ultimately determine if he lifts a prize at the end of the race. The thing that decides why one person 'does' and the other 'doesn't' is not physical ability, or the lack of it, but desire and/or the absence thereof. It is said that where there's a will there is a way, but the will doesn't exist by itself and of itself. The human will is fuelled by desire. If you have lost your desire for whatever it is you want to achieve, you've lost before you've even started. But desire alone will not accomplish all your goals for you – it is merely fuel. Imagine a car with fuel but no engine, or a car that has fuel and an engine but no wheels. It can't go anywhere! Well, it's the same if desire lacks determination, you can't move on in life.

Determination is what joins desire to commitment

Desire without determination is pointless, and determination without commitment is futile. You need all three operating together. Commitment is the key to exercising determination. You must become fully committed to a task or aim. Strong commitment will propel you onward and upward. It will motivate and inspire you, and keep you going in the face of disappointment. All high achievers have made a firm decision to stay the course – they are committed to seeing it through. Those who are unwilling to loose, rarely do! But to achieve your goals you have to set them in the first place. Setting goals shows commitment.

The starting point of any successful venture is deciding exactly what level of achievement you wish to gain. So work out on paper – for the short term, medium term and long term – exactly what you are committed to achieving. Then after you've determined how much you want to achieve, think positive, don't think of doing anything that may hinder your success. Refuse to get involved in activities that are unproductive and time-consuming. Do only what you enjoy, and what gets you the rewards you feel you're worth. And occasionally, remind yourself that you can't fly with the eagles if you continue to scratch around with the turkeys!

This observation comes from the well known motivational speaker Zig Ziglar, and it says that in order for you to become one of the best in your field, you must associate with the best in your field. Therefore, you may need to avoid the people who are going nowhere and who don't respect your time. Stay away from anyone who doesn't share your commitment to excellence. Birds of a feather, unfortunately, do flock together. So if you associate with negative people, you will likely become just as negative as them. Most top achievers tend to keep themselves separate, in order to keep themselves positive, motivated and focused on what they do. You must also discipline yourself in the same fashion. If you want to be the best, you must hang around the best. But what's more important is this – you must have true staying power!

Determination brings out the best in you

Determination will bring out the best in you, and help you defeat discouragement and disappointment. Determination is the weapon you can use to overcome temporary failure, and to prevent failure from becoming permanent. Determination produces patience and builds character. It feeds your beliefs and starves your doubts. Determination also helps you become a more reliable person because you fulfil all your commitments. It helps you prioritise and manage your time to maximise positive results.

Determination is the instrument you use to help you win in spite of your limitations Determination is the tool you use to dig yourself out of a hole.

But most important, determination is what helps you to reach your goals and fulfil your dreams.

Benjamin Franklin, is an example of a man who became successful because he mastered the art of determination. He tried over 5,000 times (and failed each time) before he was able to make the first light bulb. He could have given up after 3,000 or 4,000 tries. But winners never quit, and quitters never win. Like Benjamin Franklin, never let failure, circumstances or anyone else place limitations on your potential. With determination, you can become whatever you want to be, and achieve whatever you want to achieve.

"Success means having the courage, the determination, and the will to become the person you believe you were meant to be."

George Sheehan

PART TWO

The Law of Effective Choice

The Law of Effective Choice

Make the right choices and you'll get the right results.

"Faced with the choice between changing one's mind and proving that there is no need to do so, almost everyone gets busy on the proof."

John Kenneth Galbraith

To make the right choices you must engage your thought life correctly. Your thoughts are primary creative forces in life. You can create your entire world by the way you think. All the situations in your life have only the meaning you give them by the way you think about them. Think "happy" and you will be happy! And whenever you change your thinking, you change your life. The choice is yours. Until your thought life has changed, leaving your failings behind you is pointless. You will just end up on the same old mess. With the same old issues to deal with! However, when you consciously choose change and start thinking excellent thoughts, you will be propelled toward a balanced and prosperous life. It's time to seriously think about what you are thinking about! Stop letting those negative thoughts run riot in your mind. Learn to hold them captive. Only you have the power to dismiss them from your mind.

Almost like a magnet, we draw in what we constantly think about. If you are always thinking positive, happy, joyful thoughts, you're going to be a positive, happy, joyful person. And this will invite positive, happy and joyful situations into your life. But you must first choose to change. You need to rid yourself of negative patterns, limiting beliefs, bad habits, and doubt and unbelief. It's something only you can do. It's your life – it's your choice!

Within the Law of Effective Choice, I have discovered seven essential "right choices" we need to make – choices that will enable us to create a dynamic and balanced life. Here they are – choose to practice them.

Choose Change

"When we are no longer able to change a situation, we are challenged to change ourselves."

Victor Frankl

Changing ourselves is one of the greatest challenges we will ever face, and despite what we've been told, it's not easy. Many people often approach change as if it's something they can do without any bother but this is misleading. The main question is – could you change when change really mattered? When it mattered most? Could you change if it were a life and death situation? If you were told, "change or die," could you do it? Yes, you say! Well, you're probably deluding yourself. The chances are you wouldn't change. Do you want to know the odds? Here are the odds, the scientifically studied odds are nine to one. That's nine to one against you. How do you like those odds? Not very encouraging – are they?

In recent studies about patient behaviour, of those people questioned two years after having a coronary-artery bypass operation, an astounding 90% of them had not changed their lifestyle.

And that's been proven over and over again. So what's the missing link? Even though they know they have a very bad disease and they know they should change their lifestyle, for whatever reason, they can't. Changing behaviour isn't just the biggest challenge in health care today, it's probably the greatest challenge for us all. The central issue is never strategy, structure, culture, or systems – it's about changing the way we act. And this means reprogramming the way we think and the way we see life.

Researchers have found that certain people lived the way they did as a day-to-day strategy for coping with their emotional troubles. Therefore, telling people who are lonely and depressed that they're going to live longer if they quit smoking or change their diet and lifestyle is not that motivating. After all, some people may think, *"Who wants to live longer when I'm in chronic emotional pain?"* So instead of trying to motivate them with the "fear of dying," people are being inspired with a new vision – the "joy of living" – persuading them that they can feel better, not just live longer. That means enjoying the things that make daily life pleasurable, like starting new personal relationships, or even taking long walks without the pain caused by sickness or depression. Joy is a more powerful motivator than fear.

So what we can all learn from this study? Simply, when we choose change, let's choose change that's motivated by a joy for living. There are so many things in your life that bring you joy. Use them effectively when you need to be motivated toward positive change. For instance, if you are thinking of changing your job but you are fearful of the extra commitment that's required, think of the joy you and your family will experience when you have the money to plan and enjoy an extra holiday. I have found that whenever I focus on the joy 'change' will bring to my loved ones, I get extremely well motivated. Change is far easier to take on board when you are motivated, and at the same time, there's minimal struggle. Let joy be your strength in life, and choose to believe that tomorrow contains more joy than any of your yesterdays.

But dealing with change is never easy, and coping with change can be very stressful. I was told of a printed T-Shirt that had this sign on it: "Change is good – You start." Most of us are always looking for someone else to lead the way. Yet, it's up to you to choose change. It's up to you to be decisive, and to be decisive when confronted with change you will need to side-step your emotions and lean on acquired and processed knowledge. It's also important for you to familiarise yourself with change and get to know all its unique characteristics. Consequently, you will be able to seek change and welcome all of it's challenges.

The most significant achievements I've had in life were due to the choices I made. I chose change! I chose change when I stopped playing in a group and stared working as a record producer. I chose change when I left the music business and started my own sport sponsorship agency. I chose change when I stopped working in a church and stared a financial services company. I chose change when I folded that company to start supplying content to broadcasters. I chose change in order to set up my own TV network. And the list goes on. But there is more to change than simply changing direction.

How do you deal with change?

There are always opinions voiced concerning "change" – how important it is, and how we should alter the way we do things at work and in our personal lives in order to be more effective. Some people are convinced that it is essential to change, even if just for change's sake. However, you should be more informed about (and interested in) the process of change and what the repercussions of change really are, than how important it is to make changes.

For example, you can start by acknowledge that you exist within a contradiction. Let me explain. On the one hand, you need stability in life and perform well when you feel secure and established in your work and home life.

But on the other hand, you can become stagnant, complacent and uncreative when you avoid change or when you find you simply cannot cope with it. Therefore, there will always be a degree of tension present when dealing with change.

How can you bring these two ideas together so that you can rest easier, feel better and deal better with change? One way is for you to look closely at how limiting beliefs, negative patterns and bad habits get in the way of you being able to incorporate change into your daily life whenever it's necessary. You cannot usually predict when change will happen, but you can be better equipped to deal with it when it comes. Look seriously at the limitations you place on yourself through insecurity, fear, doubt and unbelief, and how often they hold you back from being open to change.

Try to understand how these negative patterns occur and what you can do to begin to alter them. Most people need to break the mould of tradition, unconscious habits, before any significant change can be implemented. This is where your deep rooted negative beliefs can hold you back, rather than set you free. Your belief system should create a real sense of freedom in you, and this should be evident in both your attitudes and actions. You must get to a place where you truly believe that things will change for the better, and that everything is destined to work out for your good. This view will always encourage positive change and stimulate expectancy. For expectancy brings the dream to life.

What types of changes are there?

Some change is easy to make; but more often it is difficult; and there are times when it can seem downright impossible. Essentially, there are five kinds of changes:

1. Straightforward change, like changing your house, your car, your church or even changing your hairstyle.

2. Changing something you already do and relearning a new way, like changing a skill or learning to address people differently.

3. Changing something that obviously needs changing, but you either don't want to or you can't quite see how it could be done. This kind of change usually involves a habit – for instance, smoking, drinking or gambling. You know you shouldn't be doing it, but you can't seem to stop.

4. Changing something you absolutely, positively know you can't change. This kind of change is about established, deep-rooted beliefs and it can be considered 'spiritual'.

5. Change that's imposed upon you, and over which you have no control, like loosing a loved one.

Note, the first three we wrestle with every day of our lives. We are constantly changing, but in little ways. We may struggle, yet it's usually not significant with this kind of change. Many people never completely change a bad habit, but they find it relatively easily to cope with it.

Yes, you may struggle over whether to change your car or not, but it is unlikely that changing your car is going to fundamentally change your life. A lot of other things would have to happen alongside that. It is the fourth and fifth types of change that can be the more difficult and therefore more challenging and confrontational. Both these types come right up against those deep-rooted beliefs that you've created which underpin your entire life.

For instance, the fourth type of change actually asks you to change your point of view, and adopt a way of seeing the world that's at odds with the way you are used to seeing it. This experience can easily tap into your basic insecurities. You can develop a feeling of uneasiness, a sense of not quite knowing what's the 'right' thing to do. There is no longer a predictable, reliable pattern to follow. You are challenged to step out of your comfort zone and think differently, and to most people, this is very daunting.

The fifth type, imposed change, can often come across as suffering. If you have had no say in the matter, you begin to feel victimised. You can easily feel cheated or abused. This is the hardest form of change to have to deal with. However, it can be dealt with effectively. Acceptance is the first step, after you have accepted the reality of forced change, you can learn to cope with it. It's like standing on a hilltop – all you need to do is change your view. Stop looking down into the valley and start looking at the horizon or the next peak.

When change is imposed, or when change brings us up against our established beliefs, we can easily feel disempowered by the experience. On the other hand, it is also true that some people thrive on change. But whatever your response, choosing to change is the most effective means of securing your future. It's entirely up to you! You're always free to choose. No one forces you to think, feel or behave the way you do. Rather, you choose your emotions and your behaviour by the way you choose to think about the world around you.

How you think about your circumstances and what's happening to you will determine your view of life. This is why it's so important not to limit your fundamental beliefs. Learn to think big – dream big – have big expectations.

Why is change so hard?

Neuroscience says we are pattern-making mechanisms. In general, this means that our systems are more comfortable with pattern and routine than with change. Once a pattern is established, our left-brain will quite happily keep marching along that same path. Quite simply we are creatures of habit. Most of our patterns get set very quickly; so think of the resistance you'll likely have when you try to change patterns that have been part of your life for many years.

Some patterns are as simple and straightforward as what you do first thing every morning (your routine), or the route you take into work every day.

However, other patterns are as complex as the way you feel about yourself. A good example is, the restricting or limiting patterns that are rooted in low self-esteem. These can be the hardest patterns to break. The reason being that your belief system is much stronger than the contradictory evidence you are having to face in order to change – because it's been around much longer.

Somehow you have to change the negative pattern that's been established concerning your own self-image and replace it with a better (more positive) one. How you view yourself and your own accomplishments will determine your real sense of self-worth and self-value. Low self-esteem breeds low enthusiasm, and in turn, it brings about a loss of drive and produces frustration. Such behaviour will keep you down and bound up in negativity. Unless you create a positive picture of "self" no one else can see it or enjoy it. Others will always see you as you see yourself.

Over time, parents, schooling, work mates and friends have conditioned you to think a certain way and you may have become failure conscious. Consequently, you have turned yourself into a more problem-oriented person, rather than possibility-oriented person. You instinctively focus on your weaknesses and have lost confidence and self-respect. However, when you learn to manage around your weaknesses and strengthen your strengths, you will discover a lot of "plus factors" that you didn't know you had. This starts a reversal of negative attitudes and quickly moves you toward positive self-belief and genuine enthusiasm.

You'll never rise above the image you have of yourself. So stop looking at your lacks, frailties and weaknesses and be thankful for what you've already achieved. Start celebrating your achievements – no matter how small or insignificant they may seem. Also, ask yourself two important questions... What is my self-image? And, who do I think I am? These are questions that need answered. Why? Because a healthy self-image is one of the key factors in establishing long-term success and happiness.

You are only able to speak, act and react as the person you think you are.

If, as you were growing up all you heard, over and over again, was what's wrong with you and what you need to do in order to improve yourself, then you will have a well entrenched negative belief system established. Even when you no longer have your parents and or teachers around to reinforce it, the pattern will persist. Now, they may have gone, but you still speak to yourself with that same corrective and cynical voice. Therefore, even in the face of evidence that you have achieved much, there will be this voice telling you that you could have done better.

For you to change that voice inside, you will first have to become conscious that it's actually there. Subsequently, you will have to do a good deal of "reprogramming," and in serious cases, "completely wiping the hard disc." You need to create an opposing voice of acknowledgement and praise to counterbalance the cynical or corrective voice. You must therefore start celebrating every accomplishment and reward yourself for a job well done. Also, try surrounding yourself with people that reinforce the new image you are trying to create. Praise and encouragement from others is very effective.

For some people, imposed change can often be easier to deal with. The difficulty is getting past the – "I don't want to." "It's not fair." "Why me?" – stage. Your dissatisfaction and sense of helplessness (about this type of change) came about because you didn't ever agree with it. After all, you were never consulted at the outset. So the only way through this type of change is by negotiating with yourself in order to reach agreement of some sort.

Relief from the stress and upset caused by imposed change can only be expected after you've chosen to accept and then commit to the change. This means that you must stop fighting or feeling resentful. However, if agreement with "self" is never reached, you will probably live in denial or bitterness.

The reality is, change is inevitable; and mostly change is for the good. No one lives a life free of change, but sometimes we are afflicted by more change or demands for change than we can cope with. When this happens it helps to look at what change is going to get your attention and effort.

I recommend that you look for the smallest (and simplest) change that will achieve what is needed and be wary of wholesale change – change for change's sake. Look also at yours and other people's beliefs, patterns and ways of seeing things. Changing in this area may be harder work but the end result of you changing your attitude to something can be dramatic.

The way you see things, and your view life in general, will determine your mental processes and direct your actions. And your mental processes are important enough to monitor because your life will always move in the direction of your strongest thought.

What's the matter with change?

Although many of us are generally prepared to make some changes in our current situation, and at times may even decide on more radical change like a lifestyle or behavioural adjustment, it is still part of the contradiction that people also want it to live easy, comfortable and conflict-free lives. This is because, as human beings we all have limiting beliefs, negative patterns or bad habits that will occasionally get in the way of our being able to incorporate change into our lives, or to initiate change when it is really necessary.

No one can accurately predict when change will happen, but we can be better equipped to deal with it when it comes. We should be able to create an environment where change is a natural and exciting 'organic' process.

That sounds all well and good, but how do we do it? To begin with, we can examine the limitations we all unconsciously place on ourselves, and how they hold us back from being open to change. We can try to understand how "patterns" occur and what we can do to begin altering those that are limiting or negative. And we can also look at the various kinds of changes there are and some effective ways of approaching them.

The greater our own understanding of how we are affected by change and how we react to it, the better prepared we will be to deal with it – whether that change is by our own choice or someone else's. It's important to mention once again that it is also true that some people thrive on change. They can't stay in one job, in one relationship, even in one country for very long. They somehow need to shake up their own status quo, and they often create change just for the sake of it. However, such behaviour is just as limiting as with people who find change difficult.

So don't think you can get by, or succeed, by manipulating change at random – without method, purpose or cause.

How do you cope with change

A good number of us are comfortable with the known and uncomfortable with the unknown. Therefore, change is threatening! Some, however, are genuinely seeking change and welcome its challenges. This group of people have discovered some strategies that make it easier to cope with change.

Following is a list of suggestions to help you cope with change. They may seem basic, but all are vitally important in helping make change a more positive experience.

- **Develop support relationships at work and home**. People with family and friends on whom they can rely during stressful times experience fewer negative effects of the stress change can bring. They also remain healthier, are more successful and live longer.

- **Take care of yourself**. Eat a balanced diet, exercise, and get enough rest. Take time to relax with friends and family. Enjoy your hobbies. Listen to your body, it let's you know when you need to give it more attention.

- **Build self-esteem**. There is only one you. You have special talents and interests. List what you like about yourself and note your special talents. Also, list what you appreciate about family and friends. Tell them and make them feel good, too. Praise attracts praise!

- **Be open and flexible**. Knowing that change can happen at any time helps you accept and adjust easily when it occurs. Most people are eager to settle into comfortable routines. Realise that your present routine may only be temporary. Learn to be content by accepting that everything is subject to change – but for the better!

- **Keep yourself "up on the inside."** Learn to encourage and strengthen yourself when times are tough. No one else can do it better. A positive attitude helps you to feel good about yourself, and it goes a long way toward improving your health and helps you deal with those unexpected changes that come along.

- **Take control of your life**. Practice seeing the good, or finding the positive, in each of life's changes. It's not what happens to you that causes you to be happy or unhappy; it's how you react to what happens. Your reaction governs the outcome. Take charge of your thoughts and actions. You can move away from a bad thought by deliberately moving toward a good one.

- **Remain teachable**. Use every resource available to you and keep improving through information, instruction and wise counsel. Your resources can include church life, support groups, friends, loving family members or anyone with a positive caring attitude. But learn to recognise and use them effectively.

The fundamentals of change

Some people seem to deal well with change. In fact, they seem to thrive on it. They take its challenges as sources of enormous energy to drive them forward. Like a surfer riding the face of a thundering wave, they use the power of the wave to create their own kind of strength. But there are others who just fall apart in the face of change. Things seem to go from bad to worse as they approach any form of change.

So what is the real difference between those who thrive on change and those who fall apart? Those people who thrive on change share some distinguishing qualities. They all excel in a changing environment and share these three necessary attributes:

- **Abundant Resources**: Like a family that stays out of short-term debt and builds up savings, and like a man who reaches his seventies with a body he has never abused, an organism that does not waste its resources has more options when it is threatened. In individuals, this means staying in good mental and physical health. In couples and families, it means working to keep the relationships vital and strong long before any crisis comes. And never waste your most valuable commodity – your time.

- **Abundant Relationships**: We typically constrain relationships. We form our bonds with our immediate friends and peers but we don't form strong bonds with people in the next or outer circle. Yet people who have multiple bonds and a lot of history together do better in times of difficulty. In families, this means a richness and depth of relationships, not only within the nuclear family, but beyond the family walls into the extended family, and the surrounding community. In an individual, this translates to full participation of all parts of the personality. Such a person is truly connected, committed and involved. This behaviour is usually driven by a genuine love for others.

- **Abundant Purpose**: You must develop a purpose driven life. Purpose is the fuel that drives your vision. Healthy, flexible individuals have a clear sense of purpose, and all parts of the personality are lined up behind that purpose. In healthy, flexible families, communities, and organisations, everyone has a sense of what their common endeavour is. They serve a common cause. Their past history is held in common (shared), and their future vision is developed in common.

Now that you know and understand change better, what else can you do? Since change is usually hard work, invest wisely. Aim low at first. Pick things to change that you are convinced you'll succeed at. Change is a whole lot easier when there is minimal struggle involved. Try making little tweaks and adjustments to your everyday patterns, rather than getting a completely new life. Look for things that could be fun to do – take pleasure in every moment! And keep your mind disciplined and focused on future successes. Remember, change (like life itself), should be enjoyed to the full.

Choose Consistency

"A consistent soul believes in destiny, a capricious one in chance."
Benjamin Disraeli

Being consistent is something I value greatly, and have worked hard to establish in both my personal and profession relationships. By being consistent with other people they are more likely to trust you, and trust should be at the core of all human interaction. As a husband and father, I believe that my family has been enriched in the knowledge that I've always been there for them.

When our daughter Xana was growing up, my wife Loraine and I involved her in every aspect of our lives. Even as a baby she went everywhere with us. I can honestly say we were consistent and trustworthy in how we treated her and expressed our love for her. This is why it didn't take much to discipline her. Most of the time a stern look was enough. Yes, none of us are perfect but it doesn't take perfection to become consistent, dependable and reliable.

I remember when we were staying in a plush hotel in Cyprus. Xana must have been eleven at the time and she befriended a girl about the same age. While they were playing around in the pool I started taking to the girl's father, but couldn't help noticing how unruly his son was. The boy must have been thirteen, and totally out of control. Anyway, as the days went by the two girls got so friendly that we decided to invite everyone out for a meal at a local restaurant.

At this point I would like to point out that this man was very successful. He had flown in on his own private jet. Therefore, he must have been quite influential in the business world. On with our story... Before we entered the restaurant the father decided to get some cash out of the machine at the bank opposite, so the boy and him walked over the road together. I wasn't sure what had happened but the boy started to punch and kick his dad violently. Eventually, the dad managed to pacify the boy and we sat down to have dinner. While everyone was ordering their meal my daughter Xana unknowingly started to tap her knife against a plate in front of her. I looked over and made a slight hand gesture to get her to stop. Immediately, she smiled and put the knife down. Out the corner of my eye I could see the man's reaction. It was as if I had performed a miracle! Off cause, this came up for discussion when the children weren't around a day or two later.

Both parents wanted to speak to Loraine and I about the problems they were having with their son. We then asked them how many times their son had been on holiday with them. The answer was, twice. Twice in thirteen years! You don't have to be a rocket scientist to know why the boy harboured so much anger and resentment toward his parents. He was never made to feel part of their lives. The father would get picked up by his driver at 6.00 am every morning, and he got home long after the boy was put to bed. Children want to belong, but they also need to be able to rely and depend on their parents. If a child doesn't ever know when his dad is going to be around, how can he trust him? If there isn't any consistency in the relationship the child will rebel. Consistency and stability have a profound effect on all your personal relationships. What's more, your quality of life and professional achievements will also be influenced. You can be successful and have a poor quality of life, simply because you are unstable or untrustworthy.

To become successful and achieve your goals it takes real commitment, yet it's also hard work. But what's even harder is developing the ability to maintain the same degree of success that you've worked so hard to achieve – whether it be with your family or in your business. To do this you need to establish a high level of consistency in what ever you're doing and stay in tune with a rapidly changing environment. There are many people who have achieved success only to lose it because they did not have the determination to maintain consistency. To remain successful in your career, personal life and everything else you do, you must become consistent in all your affairs. People who are consistent are usually people who can maintain the same level of performance and reliability.

Any fully developed skill, ability or talent will manifest itself in a consistent and dependable way. Have you noticed how you can always rely on your own expertise when needed? This is because your individual skills or abilities have been advanced or elaborated to a specified degree (through constant repetition) and they are now visible and trustworthy. The most fundamental aspect of proficiency is consistency because proficiency can be relied upon to deliver great results every time. That's why great sportsmen constantly produce "above the ordinary" results.

You will never attain any measure of success without being consistent at what you do. The reason being, consistency and proficiency are directly linked. Proficiency is not a destination we reach, it is an unending process of constant and consistent improvement. What better way to live than by growing better day by day? What better testimony to have than to be consistently competent? Those who pursue excellence are never in direct competition with others, because they measure themselves against their own achievements. The real contest is always between what they've done and what they believe they are capable of doing. They measure themselves against themselves and nobody else! And, they are always striving to be excellent and consistent in their chosen field.

There are six qualities that must be present if you are to become truly proficient and consistent in your endeavours. They are; **reliability, harmony, balance, agreement, enthusiasm** and **energy**. Let's examine them in detail:

Reliability

You need consistency in your life but it cannot be achieved without reliability, and as mentioned before, reliability involves trust. For most of us, things need to hang together, be predictable and make complete sense. And when they don't, we usually feel that we have a problem to solve.

Trustworthiness is almost like a law of human nature. People have a strong preference for total reliability in their lives and trust plays a big part in this (especially in personal relationships). They want things to work the same way every time they happen. When you wake up in the morning you want to find the floor under your feet, the sun above your head, and the tea in your cup. And just as you expect these kinds of physical reliabilities, you also expect psychological trust. If you have a marriage, a family, and a job today you expect to find them tomorrow in exactly the same condition.

Therefore, you have genuine expectancies about your personal world, the people in it, and your relationships with other people. But the glue that holds all these mental expectancies together is consistency – consistency founded upon reliability and trust. Why should you expect your spouse to love you tomorrow? Because it is totally consistent with your expectations. Consistency becomes like a form of human gravity – it holds everything down and together. It also helps you to understand the world and your place in it. But in the context of change, consistency allows decision making to be much less complicated and far less stressful.

Being reliable is one of the most highly sought after traits in the modern workplace. This work ethic construct includes honesty, dependability, and being on time. People who are not reliable often are very expensive to keep around because of the wasted time and resources their behaviour causes. In some cases, even peoples' lives can be seriously effected if another person is not totally reliable.

To become more reliable you can try this little exercise. Think of the various roles you engage in on any given day. For example, you may have responsibilities as a parent, a student, a worker, an athlete, a club member, a church member, or as a member of some type of team. Answer the following questions with these roles in mind. Once you have completed the questions, take a few minutes to discuss them with someone really close to you:

- What personal traits can you list that make you reliable in these roles?

- What traits would you like to develop to make you more reliable?

- What are the most important characteristics of being reliable that will help you in your future tasks, studies and/or career?

Creating a level of reliability that allows you to flourish in your personal and professional life is one element of building a better and more successful future. The ability to maintain your current level of reliability will have a major impact on tomorrow's prospects. Although, you might feel intensely devoted to your career, family or personal development, elements of your 'outer world' existence can conspire to distract you from your goals and leave you bound on a plateau that makes reliability harder to sustain. Therefore, reliability is one piece of a larger existential puzzle that puts your discipline to the test. Being reliable requires discipline because reliability's intrinsic nature is consistency.

Consistency, achieved through reliability and trustworthiness, also implies an inner integrity. To achieve consistency, you must be disciplined enough to develop and shape your desires so that they produce a kind of internal harmony. You should always be able to create harmony within yourself – an inner peace.

Harmony

There are many parts that make up the whole person – career interests, physical health, personal goals, financial state, religious beliefs, passions, problems, and so on. Harmony is a condition that comes about when all the parts of your life are balanced with each other and with the world around you.

"Perfect" balance and harmony is unnatural and never fully achievable. Think about it – no disagreement, no conflicts or problems, just a heavenly state of bliss all the time. It is the introduction of the unknown, the unexpected, the challenge of new problems, that keep life interesting. With any new endeavour will come a new challenge of some proportion. If it could be achieved effortlessly, would you have any interest in achieving it?

More often than not, the new ideas, goals and people that come into your life are not under your absolute control. They have their own motives, their own intentions and directions – and some of these will inevitably conflict with yours! If you are alive today and live on planet earth, you are going to experience a degree of disharmony. This doesn't mean you cannot achieve significant balance and harmony in your life. It means you need to choose correctly.

Personal harmony has to do with comfort and stability as this helps create a calm emotional state. Some people are never able to attain any measure of comfort. Have you ever met anyone who must have everything their own way? They live in a state of turmoil because they are not open to other people's ideas and energies. However, the other extreme is a person who fears his own goals and goes along with everyone else in an attempt to avoid conflict. Both have very narrow "comfort zones," and as a result, they become unhappy and unbalanced.

Creating harmony and balance in your life is a very personal matter. It requires tailoring your challenges (problems, conflicts, disharmonies) to your own particular "comfort zone."

A first step in achieving this is to know your own goals and intentions, and then to broaden these gradually until you create harmony. For example, let's imagine a woman who's unhappy in her love life. She feels all the good men are taken, and there just doesn't seem to be the ideal man out there for her. Because having a problem with her love life is what she uses to keep her life interesting, she feeds a lot of her time and energy into it – creating even more conflict.

This woman needs to redistribute some of her 'energy' towards a new challenge. If she suddenly found out that she had a terrible disease that required immediate medical attention, you can be sure that she would no longer be miserable about her love life. This of course, would be a challenge in the wrong direction. She would do better to consider her personal goals in another part of her life – perhaps she once had a goal to learn how to play the piano. The effort that she puts into learning something new will balance her distribution of energy and give her some new challenges (finding time to practice, understanding how to read notes, getting along with her teacher, etc) that are more tailored to her personal "comfort zone."

Notice, by now she would be more tolerant of others' imperfections (having had to deal with some of her own imperfections in meeting a new challenge) and have a broader "comfort zone." In other words, now she can find a man whose faults she can comfortably live with – after all, it is conquering new challenges that keeps life interesting! Can you see? Enjoying balance and harmony does not mean eliminating all your problems. But it does mean having the ability to distribute your time and energy appropriately to the inevitable challenges of life. Harmony is established when this is done in proportions that fit within your personal "comfort zone," which will also broaden as you take on new challenges.

Harmony provides you with more choices and allows for more areas of your life to become stable. If you consistently think in terms of maintaining harmony, you will be able to put in place additional reserves of energy, time, money or resources for those times when you are met with the unexpected. You will always have more options available to you – even when you're under pressure.

Harmony allows for flexibility and it increases your awareness of things around you. What's more, when there's harmony, you are better equipped to make wise adjustments. Even when you are in a crisis, you're able to settle yourself and bounce back quickly, having not been burdened with unnecessary stress.

To establish harmony you must step away from every negative circumstance and begin to think of the many positive aspects of your life and how they are all interrelated. Then, build in additional "faith filled" resources to cushion the unexpected. Feel confident that you can adjust fluidly to challenges. Adapt to circumstances without guilt, condemnation or judgement. Inner harmony will enable you to have more choices available to you, and therefore, no one area of your life needs to take the brunt of the additional strain of life's unexpected challenges. Begin to 'think' harmony and you'll quickly see how this attitude affects the choices you make. Remember, harmony and consistency work together to bring about happiness, peace and satisfaction.

Harmony can be defined as an agreement in feeling, approach, and sympathy. It is the pleasing interaction between what you think, feel, say, and do. But balance cannot be ignored when you are trying to produce consistency in an environment of harmony.

Balance

Balance is defined as equanimity, satisfactory distribution of elements, general soundness, or a calm emotional condition. It is a state of emotional and rational stability in which you are at peace and able to make sound decisions and judgements.

One of the most amazing insights from recent research is that when the mind is in a balanced state, the brain functions in a measurably balanced way. As you watch the electrical activity of your brain displayed on a colour monitor, you can see how moment to moment the mind / brain state flows in and out of balance.

When the brain comes into balance, there is a "syncing up" of the activity of both the left and right sides of the brain. It is like what happens when dozens of individual musicians stop tuning their individual instruments, or stop trying to drown each other out, and finally begin to actually play music together as one orchestra. Good orchestration always takes into account balance and harmony.

Too much of one thing is never advisable, and this is the same with everything we do in life. Too much work upsets the balance between you and your family. Too much creative thinking without any action, upsets the balance between creativity and productivity.

A healthy, well-balanced mind comes as a product of an understanding of yourself, others and life acquired by reflective thought, observation and "experience with life". It arises out of the a thoughtful, intelligent, rational, inquiring, questioning mind – a mind that is able to think for itself and come to its own opinions and conclusions.

A mind that can evaluate itself correctly, as well as keep the balance necessary to establish emotional and rational stability. Here are seven things you can do to help balance your life:

1. **Slow Down**. Life is simply too short, so don't let things pass you by. Take steps to stop and enjoy the things and people around you. Schedule more time between meetings; don't make plans for every evening or weekend, and find some ways to distance yourself from the things that are causing you the most stress.

2. **Learn to Better Manage Your Time – Avoid Procrastination**. For many people, most of the stress they feel comes from simply being disorganised – and procrastinating. Learn to set more realistic goals and deadlines – and then stick to them. You'll find that not only are you less stressed, but your work will be better.

3. **Share the Load**. Even though we may sometimes feel we're the only ones capable of doing something, it's usually not the case. Get your partner or other family members to help you with all your personal/ family responsibilities. Taking care of the household, children, or parents should not be the responsibility of just one person.

4. **Let Things Go (Don't Sweat the Small Stuff)**. It's simpler said than done! But learn to let things go every once in a while. So what if the car isn't washed every week or that the house doesn't get vacuumed

regularly. Learn to recognise the things that don't really have much impact on your life and allow yourself to let them go – and then don't beat yourself up for doing so.

5. **Explore Your Options – Get Help**. If you are feeling overwhelmed with your family or work responsibilities, get help. Find a solution for dealing with your children, explore options for ageing parents, and seek counselling for yourself if necessary. In most cases, you have options, but you need to take the time to find them.

6. **Take Charge – Set Priorities**. Sometimes it's easier for us to allow ourselves to feel overwhelmed rather than taking charge and developing a prioritised list of things that need to get done. You must be determined to change this trend. Develop a detailed list. Set clear priorities. And then enjoy the satisfaction of crossing things off your list.

7. **Simplify**. It seems the norm for just about everyone to take on too many tasks and responsibilities, to try to do too much, and to own too much. Find a way to simplify your life. Change your lifestyle. Learn to say no to requests from people who waist your time. Get rid of the clutter in your house – and your life.

In the end, the key word is balance. You need to find the right balance that works for you. Celebrate your successes and don't dwell on your failures. Life is a process, and so is striving for balance in your life. Harmony and balance are perhaps the most important qualities of all when you are seeking consistency, for they serve as building blocks for the remaining qualities. When you have established harmony and balance, what you think, say, feel, and do is in total agreement.

People today are so accustomed to this split-screen state of mind in which they think one thing and say another, feel something else, and act in a way that has nothing to do with what they have just thought, said, or felt. This, is an unbalanced state. When your thoughts, feelings, words, and actions are not in harmony, it shows up as an imbalance – you feel agitated and uncomfortable, so you find it difficult to make rational, calm decisions. This is why these two qualities are an inseparable pair. There is a lot of inner strength available to you when your heart and mind are in total agreement.

Therefore, consistency involves both balance and harmony, but is dependent on "agreement" between your head and your heart – your reasoning and your emotions must be fully compatible.

Agreement

You can never be compatible or in agreement with anyone or anything if you are inconsistent. This unstable state effects every area of your life – especially your relationship with others. There may have been times in your relationships with others where you probably wish you would have listened to your head, and not your heart. Yet there are other times when you may have wished just the opposite! So when your head and your heart seem to be leading you in opposite directions – how do you know which one to listen to? If I think of two friends disagreeing over a subject, most probably I can see that both of them have only a slice of the whole picture.

When they combine their efforts and experience, and search for what they don't know about the subject, they are often able to come to an agreement that satisfies them both. Maybe the heart and head work in the same way. Each part of us is able to give its share of insight, and when they seem to disagree, it might be that they need to search for more of the complete picture. You've probably found that your best decisions come when your heart and head are in harmony, instead of disagreement.

Today, if your heart is telling you one thing, and your head seems to be leading you in a different direction, remind yourself that maybe you're not ready to make a good decision yet (on whatever you are struggling with). Rather, begin to look closely at the areas where your heart and head differ, and see if you can get more insight in order to bring them into agreement. The desires in your heart and the reasoning of your mind must agree. Too many of us are quick to figure out what we want but don't have the desire to see it through.

Enterprising go-getters have an intense desire to advance themselves, and they have a clear vision of a better future which they are determined to realise. Their heads and their hearts are always in agreement with their vision. There is never any conflict between the intellect and the emotions to deal with. They have found peace of mind and established peace in the heart.

But how can we avoid conflict between the intellect and our emotions? First, we must accept that training the intellect does not result in intelligence. Rather, intelligence comes into being when we act in perfect harmony, both intellectually and emotionally. There is a vast distinction between intellect and intelligence. Intellect is merely thought functioning independently of emotion (heart). When intellect, irrespective of emotion, is trained in any particular direction, we may have great intellect, but we do not have intelligence, because in intelligence there is the inherent capacity to feel as well as to reason. In true intelligence both intellect and emotion are equally present – intensely and harmoniously.

Modern education focuses on developing the intellect, offering more and more explanations, more and more theories, without the harmonious quality of love and affection. Therefore, we have developed clever minds in order to escape from this conflict – becoming satisfied with explanations that scientists and philosophers give us. The mind – the intellect – is totally comfortable with these innumerable explanations, but intelligence is not, for to truly understand there must be complete unity of mind and heart in action. According to this principle, when you have established agreement between heart and mind, you gain understanding, and you will then be able to demonstrate a high level of true intelligence. Out of this intelligence flows fresh energy – a tangible measure of enthusiasm.

Enthusiasm

Enthusiasm feeds consistency simply because it has energy and momentum. There is something truly magnetic and attractive about a happy and enthusiastic person. Most of us are drawn to people who are consistently "up" – people that are stimulating and exhilarating to be around. What they possess is absorbing and contagious. I love the story of Tom Sawyer, who as a young boy was told to go outside and paint the fence. Like most young lads, Tom wasn't that keen on working. He would rather go out and play with his friends. But instead of getting disgruntled he decided to make the best of that situation. So he went out and started to paint the fence with great enthusiasm and excitement (as though he was really enjoying it).

When Tom's friends came round and saw that he was having so much fun painting the fence, they became envious of him. Their response was, *"Hey, Tom! Would you let us try painting that fence?" "Oh, no."* Tom replied, *"This is my fence. This is my project. You could never do what I am doing."* He played it up real big. And you probably know how the story ends. When it was all done and dusted, Tom Sawyer was left sitting back watching his friends do all the work.

Notice, because Tom had decided to approach the chore with excitement and enthusiasm, his friends couldn't resist getting involved. Enthusiasm is like a magnet, it draws people's attention.

In a recent study on Leadership Traits, hundreds of successful leaders from all walks of life (and in various different professions), were examined to find out what they all shared in common. There were many good qualities shared by large groups of people but only one that all great leaders possessed – enthusiasm! Think about it... Would you follow someone who is cynical and unenthusiastic?

The word enthusiasm is derived from the Greek word, 'enthusiasms', which means to be inspired or possessed by a divine being. Enthusiasm is an incredibly powerful tool to create momentum. Enthusiasm can also be used to combat fear and nervousness and it can even provide energy and willpower. Being enthusiastic also creates an overall feeling of happiness and well-being that makes having it worthwhile, regardless of its positive side-effects. However, so many people have become unenthusiastic and timid. The media is constantly barraging it's audiences with messages of tragedy, pessimism and fear. In such an environment it's probably more common to side with cynicism and sarcasm than enthusiasm.

Generally, people in western society are apathetic, so we naturally adapt to these kinds of behaviours, largely without realising that we are doing it. With so much negativity around, how can we possibly hope to cultivate the kind of enthusiasm we need to succeed? Enthusiasm is like any other skill. If it is continually practised and exercised, it gets better. If it is not, then it will degrade. Enthusiasm rarely comes naturally – it must be the result of conscious effort. Practising the ability to use enthusiasm can keep you excited and driven even in negative circumstances. Without this ability even great situations are viewed through the lens of sarcasm and cynicism. We need to harness our own inner strength – we need enthusiasm!

Genuine enthusiasm can only be sustained around something you are truly passionate about. Anyone can get themselves hyped up over a boring situation for the moment, but sustained enthusiasm can only come when you deeply care about something. If you aren't that interested in the outcome of something, you won't be able to create enthusiasm. Don't spend your time pursuing things that you aren't passionate about. If you aren't passionate about something, try to minimise or remove the time it is taking from your life. Nobody is going to applaud you for working at a boring job, having boring hobbies or staying in a dead relationship. Passion will always get you to do something about it!

If you look at really successful people, all of them have something they are very passionate about. Such people have a drive that compels them to give 110%. Nothing is more motivating than focused passion. Passion provides the fuel, without it there can be no fire of enthusiasm. Being enthusiastic requires a lot more of your energy, but at the same time it creates more energy. If you're feeling like passing out from exhaustion at the end of each day, chances are you aren't brimming with excitement. Enthusiasm and energy are very closely linked. Being energetic makes it far more likely for you to be enthusiastic, and enthusiasm can literally create the energy you need to get moving.

Energy

When you are able to take more control of your emotions, you can improve the quality of your energy, regardless of the external pressures you are facing. To do this, you must first become more aware of how your are feeling at various points during the day and of the impact these emotions are having on your effectiveness and performance. Most people realise that they tend to perform best when they're feeling positive energy. What they find awkward is that they're not able to perform well or effectively when they're feeling any other way.

One simple but very powerful practice that defuses negative emotions and fuels positive emotions is expressing appreciation to others. This is a practice that seems as beneficial to the giver as to the one receiving. It can take the form of a hand-written note, an e-mail, a phone call, or a face to face conversation – and the more detailed and specific the higher the impact. Why not make an effort to show and demonstrate your appreciation to those around you regularly?

Another way to cultivate positive emotions, and in turn create more energy, is by learning to change the stories you tell yourself about the events in your life. Often, people in conflict cast themselves into the role of victim, blaming others or external circumstances for all their problems. Becoming aware of the difference between the facts in any given situation and the way you interpret those facts can be powerful in itself.

It's been a revelation to many people I have counselled over the years. When they discover that they actually have a choice about how they view a given event in their lives, it liberates them. They are also encouraged to recognise how powerfully the story they tell themselves influences their emotions. I then teach them to tell the most hope-filled and personally empowering story possible in any given situation, without denying or minimising the facts.

The most effective way you can change a story is to view it through any of three new "life lenses." These lenses are viable alternatives to seeing the world from the victim perspective, and each lens can help you intentionally cultivate more positive emotions.

- **The reverse lens**. The reverse lens allows you to ask yourself, *"What would the other person in the conflict say and in what ways might that be true?"*

- **The long lens**. Wearing the long lens you ask, *"How will I most likely view this situation in six months time?"*

- **The wide lens**. With the wide lens you ask yourself, *"Regardless of the outcome of this issue, how can I grow and learn from it?"*

Nicolas Bablin, director of communications for Sony Europe, was the point person for calls from reporters when Sony went through several recalls of its batteries in 2006. Over time he found his work increasingly exhausting and downright discouraging. After practising the "life lenses" exercise, he began to find way of telling himself a more positive and empowering story about his role. "I realised," he explains, that this was an opportunity for me to build stronger relationships with journalists by being fully accessible to them and to increase Sony's credibility by being straightforward and honest." Nicolas Bablin changed the story he was telling himself, but he also acted in a way consistent with his beliefs.

People tap into the energy of the human spirit when their everyday work and activities are consistent with their beliefs. In particular, what they value most and what gives them a sense of meaning and purpose. If what you are doing really matters to you, typically you will feel more positive energy, focus better and demonstrate greater perseverance. To access the energy of the human spirit, you need to clarify your core beliefs and establish a good value system. Thereafter, do what you do best and enjoy what you are doing! You deserve it!

Choose Competence

"Excellence can be obtained if you:

> *care more than others think is wise;*
>
> *risk more than others think is safe;*
>
> *dream more than others think is practical;*
>
> *and expect more than others think is possible."*

(Unknown writer)

In our search for excellence we must first discover our strengths and weaknesses. We should develop a good understanding of our natural gifts and abilities. I am fully convinced that every one of us has a distinct and unique assortment talents. The problem is that the majority of us never get to know what they are, and if we do, we never get to nurture and develop them to a point where they can prospers us. In other words, we never become truly competent within our strengths.

Someone once said, *"competence is the ability to use your natural strengths on a consistent basis."* But core competency is different. It is fundamental knowledge, ability, or expertise in a specific subject area or skill set.

For example, an individual who becomes certified as a Microsoft Certified Software Engineer is said to have a core competency in certain

Microsoft systems and networks. Companies with specific strengths in the marketplace, such as data storage or the development of accounting applications, can be said to have a core competency in that area. The core part of the term indicates that the individual has a strong basis from which to gain the additional competence to do a specific job or that a company has a strong basis from which to develop additional products.

Accomplishment is a deliberate act

Competency begins when you know that being good won't carry the day, when doing more or trying harder won't bridge the gap, when excellence is simply the only alternative. Accomplishment is deliberate, not an accident that we stumble upon. It is about asking of ourselves more than others do; it is about harbouring thoughts of success in our hearts.

As long as we aim for a more ideal self, success will naturally follow. And the good news is that competency and proficiency are within the grasp of all of us, for they are merely about doing our best at every moment. It is not about perfection, which is an unattainable goal, but about becoming what we are capable of being with our existing skills.

You can increase your efficiency and your effectiveness by becoming better and better at your key tasks. One of the most powerful of all time management techniques is for you to get better at the most important things you do. That is, your core competencies, your key skills, or the places and areas that you excel. These key elements will determine the level of success you can achieve in life.

Your great responsibility in life is to determine what things you can and should do very well and then to develop a plan to become excellent in those vital areas.

Your weakest important skill sets the standard at which you can use all your other skills. So be painfully honest with yourself. What is your most limiting skill? What is the one skill that determines the speed at which you complete your major tasks? What is the one skill – the lack of which may be holding you back? The underachiever always looks for a reason for his or her problems in the outer world. But the high achiever looks within. Such a person will always ask, "What is it in me that's holding me back?"

Successful people are very self-aware – they look inside to find the answers and get solutions to their problems. Unsuccessful people are always trying to find someone or something to blame.

Don't get caught up in this spiral of negative thought and bad attitudes. Move quickly from positive thinking to positive knowing. From wishing and hoping, to a total conviction that you can do anything you put your mind to. Then, seek to find that one and most important skill, that if it was developed and performed in an excellent fashion, would have the greatest positive impact on your future. You will be absolutely amazed at the difference this will make.

See yourself as an extraordinary person, with talents and abilities far beyond anything you have ever accomplished in the past. You are living in your golden years where more achievements are possible – more than you've ever imagined. There are no limits on what you can do except the limits you place on your own mind.

Excellence is a lifestyle

Those who stand by the sidelines and watch others succeed, know what is necessary, but are unwilling to devote the time and effort to bettering themselves.

So, each of us has to make a decision. Do we wish to become another statistic by merging with the mediocre majority or do we wish to make a difference by embracing excellence?

Some people rationalise it by telling themselves that they will strive for excellence later, when they have a better job, a better opportunity, more money, etc. They try to conceal from themselves the fact that better jobs, greater opportunities and more money only come after attaining a level of excellence, not the other way around. "Why should I do my best now," they argue, "when all I'm doing is flipping burgers, cleaning toilets, or waiting on others?" Perhaps they don't realise there are no dead-end jobs, only dead-end-kids; there are no menial jobs, only menial attitudes. For as Martin Luther King Jr. said, *"If a man is called to be a street sweeper, he should sweep streets even as Michelangelo painted, or Beethoven composed music, or Shakespeare wrote poetry. He should sweep streets so well that all the hosts of heaven and earth will pause to say, here lived a great street sweeper who did his job well."*

Today, we expect to find high quality merchandise and good service in any department store. However, it wasn't always that way. In the nineteenth century, unethical merchandising practices and shoddy merchandise were the rule of the day. However, Marshall Field (1834 ~ 1906) believed in excellence. When he established Marshall Field and Company in 1881, he introduced credit, the one-price system, the right to return merchandise, and a department store restaurant for shoppers.

Here in his own words are his ideas about excellence: *"To do the right thing, at the right time, in the right way; to do some things better than they were ever done before; to eliminate errors; to know both sides of the question; to be courteous; to be an example; to work for the love of work; to anticipate requirements; to develop resources; to recognise no impediments; to master circumstances; to act from reason rather than rule; to be satisfied with nothing short of perfection."*

Although I've been using examples of competence and excellence in the business world, the art of doing our best applies to every aspect of life. Or in the words of James A. Michener, *"The master in the art of living makes little distinction between his work and his play, his labour and his leisure, his mind and his body, his information and his recreation, his love and his religion. He hardly knows which is which. He simply pursues his vision of excellence at whatever he does, leaving others to decide whether he is working or playing. To him he's always doing both."*

Those who are successful in their quest for great accomplishment simply do what they do better and do more of it. They go about life always alert for better ways of doing things. Every endeavour they engage in is imprinted with their mark of excellence. They understand that if you do a job quickly, people will forget about it. But if you do it well, people will remember. They believe that if you consistently do your best, the worst won't happen. Here's some good advice for us from the Founder of IBM, Thomas J. Watson (1874 ~ 1956), "If you want to achieve excellence, you can get there today. As of this second, quit doing less-than-excellent work."

Excellence has to do with attitude

Excellence is not a matter of ability, knowledge or practice. It cannot be taught, imposed, or wished into existence. Excellence is a matter of the attitude we have and the stand we take — a stand that allows for a performance that surpasses what was previously possible, performance that defies old limits and maps out new territory. All of us have had moments when we've succeeded seemingly without effort, times when we've performed superbly and gracefully, times when we've hit the mark. Yet we are never quite sure how it all came together, how it happened, or if we can make it happen again. This may be an experience on the road to excellence, but it's not our destination. When we have overtaken mediocrity, there is always a degree of certainty (consistency), and the long road ahead is clearly visible.

The journey to truly superior performance is neither for the faint-hearted nor for the impatient. New research shows that outstanding performance is the product of many years of deliberate practice and coaching, and not necessarily of any innate talent or skill. Suggesting that experts are made and not born.

Without doubt, the amount and quality of practice are key factors in the level of expertise you can achieve, but this may be misleading because there must be something there for you to work on in the first place. Therefore, even though excellence may not result directly out of any innate talent or skill, it will still require some innate talent of skill from which to build.

Hard work and natural ability go hand in hand and correlate with success. All superb performers are gifted, but they have also studied with devoted teachers, practised intensely, and have probably been supported by their families throughout their developing years.

The development of genuine expertise requires much sacrifice. There are no short cuts. It will probably take you at lease a decade to achieve superior performance in your chosen field. And you will need to invest that time wisely, by engaging in "deliberate" practice – practice that focuses on tasks beyond your current level of competence and comfort. You will need a well informed instructor not only to guide you through deliberate practice but also to help you learn how to coach yourself. Remember, it takes time to become an expert. In sport even the most gifted performers need a minimum of ten years of intense training before they win international competitions.

Excellence is hard work

To many people the dreaming is more exciting than the doing. They want to find an effortless way to achieve their goals. This microwave mentality is very popular but completely unproductive. You can stand in a garage for as long as you like but you'll never come out a car, and living in a cave does not make you a geologist! To fulfil your dream it's going to take hard word, dedication and much practice. And you will need a particular kind of practice – deliberate practice – if you are to become excellent in your field. When most people practice they focus on the things they already know how to do. Deliberate practice is different. It involves specific and sustained efforts to do something you can't do that well. It entails controlled and deliberate repetition with a precise goal in mind.

When playing golf you don't improve simply because you are competing in a game. You get only a single change to make a shot from any location. You don't get to figure out how you can correct your mistakes. However, if you were allowed to take ten (or more) shots from the exact location on the course, you would be able to adjust your playing technique to improve your control. In fact, professional golfers often take multiple shots from the same location when they train and when they check out a course before a tournament. This form of practice – deliberate practice – will prove invaluable in any activity or profession. However, moving outside your comfort zone of achievement requires substantial motivation and sacrifice, yet it's a necessary discipline.

As the golf champion Sam Snead once put it, *"It's only human nature to want to practice what you can already do well, since it's a hell of a lot less work, and much more fun."* Only when you see that deliberate practice is the most effective means to the desired end – becoming the best in your field – will you commit to excellence. Deliberate practice is the key to your success. Sam Snead said, *"It puts brains in your muscles!"*

Excellence thinks deliberate thoughts

Genuine experts not only practice deliberately they also think deliberately. Another golfer Ben Hogan once explained, *"While I am practising I am also trying to develop my powers of concentration. I never just walk up and hit the ball."* Hogan decided in advance where he wanted the ball to go and how to get it there. It's the same when it comes to achieving success in your own life.

Your thought patterns must be deliberate and methodical, and you levels of concentration and dedication must be high. But when practising, be careful not to overdo it. It's interesting to note that across a wide range of experts, including athletes, novelists and musicians, very few were able to engage in more than four or five hours of high concentration and deliberate practice at any one time.

Someone once said, *"God does not want us to do extraordinary things. He wants us to do ordinary things extraordinary well."* When we start practising deliberately we will be able to do everyday things in an exceptional way, and everyone will sit up and take notice. If you want to stand out in the crowd, all you need to do is practice more, and work harder and longer than anyone else. For many people, a lack of integrity and mediocrity is the norm. They want to do as little as possible, in a haphazard way, and still get the rewards they desire. Such people will never experience the pleasure of doing a job right and doing it to the best of their ability. Wholeheartedness is a characteristic of excellence and it is appreciated by all.

You need to cultivate integrity and excellence as a way of life. This means going beyond the normal call of duty, stretching your perceived limits and holding yourself responsible for becoming the best (and giving your best). It means maintaining the highest standards, paying attention to every little detail and being willing to go the extra mile to get the job done. After all, you are always on display, whether you realise it or not. The eye is a better observer and much sharper than the ear. So stop "talking the talk" and start doing what needs to be done! Most people will read you better than you read yourself.

Greatness lives inside of you

I'm convinced that in today's competitive world we need more people who aspire to attain some measure of greatness, and not merely people who desire to be successful. In the larger picture, success is a weak relative of greatness because generally human success desires to make a lot of money in order to stop working. But greatness sets out to change, or at the very least, improve the world in which it lives. The question we should all ask ourselves is this, *"Am I seeking success for success sake, or do I genuinely want to make an impact and become influential?"*

When confronted with such a daunting challenge, it's probably a lot easier to make excuses and align yourself to mediocrity. But greatness is evidenced by excellence but preceded by integrity. Greatness (which is always preceded by integrity) involves a large degree of sacrifice. What's more, pursuing greatness will upset every tidy plan you've ever made, and may even put you at risk. Therefore, greatness is not for the fainthearted.

Genuine greatness will always choose to rise above the mediocrity that surrounds it and strive for excellence at any cost. Greatness requires resolve (true grit), and it has genuine staying power. It means going the extra mile for what is right. It means keeping your word even when it hurts. If you want to make an impact, start aiming for excellence and integrity. Start aiming for greatness! Seek to be prominent in your assigned or nominated area of expertise. Why shouldn't you become world renown for what you do? See yourself being influential and well-thought-of. This may not necessarily be raw ambition, for it may be the true spark of greatness within you.

But where are our great leaders today? Where are the present day heroes? Where can we find that new breed of illustrious champions? The truth is, we can all answer the call to greatness. Greatness is already present in each of us. But it needs to be mined like a precious stone, and then polished and properly set into our lives. This will require time and dedication, and it may cause us some heartache as well. Greatness is not a cheap commodity. William Shakespeare said, "Greatness knows itself." (Henry 1V, Part 1 –1597).

Seven things you can do

Seven things you can do (to rise above mediocrity and ascend into greatness):

1. **Have a real sense of destiny**. There is an interesting story in the Bible that has always inspired me. When Josiah became king, he was only eight years old. Right up until his mid-twenties he wrestled with his identity. He had an identity crisis and lacked the soil in which to cultivate greatness. This man had the worst family tree you can ever imagine. His grandfather, Manassah, was the most renowned mass murderer of God's prophets, and his father, Ammon, was a moral sewer rat.

    Josiah became king because of an assassination, and therefore, there was no one to mentor him. Yet he became the most powerful and zealous religious reformer in Jewish history. In fact, he did more to remove witchcraft, idols, and cultural sin (in the shortest span of time) then any other king in the Bible. How could this be?

    The answer lies in a mysterious prophecy given 355 years before Josiah was born. But it all came together when the desecrated temple in Jerusalem was being renovated. An old book was found and it was delivered to the king. There, contained in this ancient document was Josiah's true identity. He read it and the effect was astonishing. It instantly solved his personality crisis, and he discovered his destiny. Immediately, Josiah tore his clothes, roared like a lion, and went into a frenzy of righteousness. This instant vision of greatness drove him to cleanse an entire nation. Once Josiah had clearly seen his destiny and had understood who he really was, he rose to true greatness!

2. **Chart a bold and original course**. So many of us are too predictable – it's almost embarrassing. Who cares if you never did it this way before! If you're going to get away from that well-worn path and venture out onto the highway of greatness, you must cultivate brave new ideas. You need to become that person in society that is least threatened by new ideas, by experimentation and by taking risks. So write down the your vision clearly; crowning each sentence with *"I can do it,"* and at the same time, making sure that it has the aroma of the extraordinary. I believe in the old saying, *"If you reach for the sky you will probably touch the clouds."*

3. **Do more – on a broader scale – and not less**. The narrower your thinking becomes, the less you will be able to accomplish. The truth is, more often than not, those who open their hearts to do more actually accomplish more in every area. It's up to you to expand and enlarge your heart. This experience is liberating and it will make you more open and receptive to doing and enjoying life. After all, greatness reflects a character that loves living – and living life to the full.

4. **Choose not to mingle with mediocrity**. What you accept or tolerate in your life will influence your future. The Bible says, *"A righteous man should choose his friends carefully."* You should purpose to hang around with positive (inspirational) people, and your inner circle must be made up of friends who challenge you to greatness. They should be optimistic 'self-starters' with real integrity. People who strive for excellence no

matter what. Pessimists will wear you down, and emotional parasites will eat up your time and deplete your dreams.

5. **Develop tenacity**. The difference between winning or loosing is simply giving up! All the talent, opportunity and money in the world cannot compete with stubborn persistence in the creation of greatness. Always go the extra mile and make the extra effort – when it counts most. In you "right now" is staying power. When you tap into this inner strength you will always find that little bit extra, that little bit of super-glue. So stick with it! Don't give up on any of your dreams.

6. **Closely guard your dream**. Today's society is designed to enhance and serve the half-hearted, the slothful and the greedy. So don't let this system threaten your passion, growth and courage. Study your dream closely; polish your vision regularly; and never take your eyes off the winning post. Then, always remember to weed out tendencies within and without which may erode your pursuit of excellence. Your greatness is securely contained in your dream and your dream is surrounded by excellent pursuits (great ideas and great plans).

7. **Never ripen**. Always remain enthusiastic, passionate, interested and teachable. Don't just go through the motions in life, be keen to learn and experience more and more. The more experience you gain the quicker your character will grow. Character flourishes in the tests and trials of life because that's exactly where it is best developed. Mediocrity looks for the quickest way to retirement, but greatness never does. Great soldiers can't retire or draw back while there is still new territory to occupy. So remind yourself every day to stay involved, stay hungry, and stay excited!

It's Your Life, It's Your Choice

Choose Confidence

"Put your future in good hands - your own."

Author Unknown

Self-confidence is an attitude which allows you to have positive yet realistic views of yourself and your situations. Self-confident people trust their own abilities. They have a general sense of control in their lives, and believe that, within reason, they will be able to do what they wish, plan, and expect. Having self-confidence does not mean that you will be able to do everything.

Self-confidence makes your expectations more realistic. Even when some of your expectations are not met, you continue to be positive and accept yourself as you are. People who are not self-confident depend excessively on the approval of others in order to feel good about themselves. They tend to avoid taking risks because they fear failure. They generally do not expect to be successful. They often put themselves down and would rather discount or ignore compliments paid to them.

By contrast, self-confident people are willing to risk the disapproval of others because they generally trust their own abilities. They accept themselves at every level, and they don't feel they have to conform in order to be accepted.

Self-confidence is not necessarily a general characteristic which pervades all aspects of your life. Typically, you will have some areas where you feel quite confident, while at the same time you may not feel at all confident in other areas. Self-confidence is extremely important in almost every aspect of life, yet so many people struggle to find it. Sadly, this can be a vicious circle. People who lack self-confidence can find it difficult to become high achievers. Mainly because they don't get a positive response from others. After all, would you instinctively want to back a project that was being presented by someone who was nervous, fumbling and overly apologetic? On the other hand, you might be persuaded to get involved by someone who spoke clearly, who held their head high, who answered questions assuredly, and who readily admitted when he/she did not know something.

Self-confidence inspires confidence in others – their audience, their peers, their bosses, their customers, and their friends. Gaining the confidence of others is one of the primary ways in which a self-confident person finds success. The good news is – self-confidence can be learned and built on. And, whether you're working on your own self-confidence or building the confidence of people around you, it's well-worth the effort! All other things being equal, self-confidence is often the single ingredient that distinguishes a successful person from someone less successful.

How is Self-Confidence Initially Developed?

Many factors affect the development of self-confidence. Parents' attitudes are crucial to children's feelings about themselves, particularly in children's early years. When parents provide acceptance, children receive a solid foundation for good feelings about themselves.

If one or both parents are excessively critical or demanding, or if they are overprotective and discourage moves toward independence, children may come to believe they are incapable, inadequate, or inferior. However, if parents encourage children's moves toward self-reliance and accept and love their children when they make mistakes, children will learn to accept themselves and will be on their way to developing self-confidence.

Surprisingly, lack of self-confidence is not necessarily related to lack of ability. Instead it is often the result of focusing too much on the unrealistic expectations or standards of others, especially parents and society. Friends' influences can be as powerful, or more powerful, than those of parents (and society) in shaping feelings about one's self. Students in their college years re-examine values and develop their own identities and therefore, are particularly vulnerable to the influence of friends. This is why we must be careful who we hang around with. Go where you're celebrated, not where you're tolerated!

How do you create a sense of balanced self-confidence?

Self-confidence is being certain (and trusting) about yourself with regards to addressing certain tasks or other people. Self-confidence is critical to effective performance in the workplace and in the home, and it is the source of assertiveness – which is fully representing yourself (your opinions, recommendations, etc) to others. But self-confidence is also about balance. At one extreme, we have people with low self-confidence. At the other end, we have people who may be overconfident. Good self-confidence is a matter of having the right amount of confidence, founded in reality and on your true abilities. With the right amount of self-confidence, you will take informed risks, stretch yourself (but not go beyond your strengths and abilities) and try harder.

By contrast, if you are under-confident, you'll avoid taking risks and stretching yourself; and you might not try at all. This means that you'll fail to reach your full potential.

And if you're overconfident, you'll probably take too much risk, stretch yourself beyond your capabilities, and fail badly. You may also find that you're too optimistic, or that you don't try hard enough to gain success. So, self-confidence needs to be founded on reality – realistic expectations. That is, your present skills and experience, and the effort and preparation that you are willing to put in to reach your goal.

So how do you build this sense of balanced self-confidence – founded on a firm appreciation of reality? The bad news is that there's no quick fix. The good news is that building self-confidence is readily achievable, just as long as you have the focus and determination to carry things through. And what's even better is that the things you do will make you successful. After all, your confidence will come from real, solid achievement. No-one can take this away from you!

So... How do you do it? Here are a few suggestions:

1. **Build the knowledge you need to succeed**: Looking at your goals, identify the skills you'll need to achieve them. And then look at how you can acquire these skills confidently and well. Don't just accept a sketchy, just-good-enough solution – look for a solution, a program or a course that fully equips you to achieve what you want to achieve, and ideally gives you a qualification you can be proud of. Investing in knowledge and skills, is a sound investment in your future.

2. **Focus on the basics**: When you're starting to build self-confidence, don't try to do anything clever, too ambitious or elaborate. And don't reach for perfection – just enjoy doing simple, straightforward things successfully and well. Getting used to being an achiever means getting used to finishing everything you've started.

3. **Set small goals, and accomplish them**: Start with the small goals that you've identified, and then get into the habit of achieving them and celebrating that achievement. Don't make goals particularly challenging at the beginning, just get into the habit of accomplishing them and celebrating them. And little by little, start piling up the successes!

4. **Keep managing your mind**: Stay on top of that positive thinking, keep celebrating and enjoying success, and keep those mental success images strong. And on the other side, learn to handle failure. Accept that mistakes happen when you're trying something new. In fact, if you get into the habit of treating mistakes as learning experiences, you can start to see them in a positive light. After all, there's a lot to be said for the saying "if it doesn't kill me, it'll make me stronger!" And remember to keep yourself grounded – this is where people tend to get overconfident and over-stretch themselves. So make sure you don't start enjoying cleverness for its own sake!

5. **Avoid self-defeating thought patterns**: Subscribing to negative assumptions leaves you vulnerable to the following self-defeating thought patterns:

   • **All or Nothing Thinking**. Thinking that you're a failure because your performance was not perfect.

   • **Seeing Only Dark Clouds**. Thinking that disaster lurks around every corner and then it comes it's to be expected. For example, a single negative detail, piece of criticism, or passing comment darkens all your reality.

   • **Magnification of the Negative / Minimisation of the Positive**. In your life, good things don't count nearly as much as the bad ones. Your glass is always half empty.

   • **Uncritical Acceptance of Emotions as Truth**. Whenever you feel inadequate, you think it must be true. But feelings are not the truth!

   • **Labelling**. Labelling is a simplistic process and often conveys a sense of blame. Confessing things like, "I am a loser, and, it's my fault," or, "Things never go right for me anyway – I attract disaster."

- **Difficulty Accepting Compliments**. When you are given a compliment, you are quick to nullify it. For example, "So you like this outfit? I think it makes me look fat," or, "I'm glad you like my presentation, however, I'm never good at expressing myself."

Strategies for Developing Confidence

- **Emphasise Your Strengths**. Give yourself credit for everything you attempt. By focusing on what you can do well, you applaud yourself for efforts rather than emphasising end results. Start from a base of where your strengths are located, this helps you live within the bounds of your inevitable limitations.

- **Take Risks**. Approach new experiences as fresh opportunities to learn rather than occasions to win or lose. Doing so opens you up to new possibilities and can increase your sense of self-acceptance. Not doing so turns every possibility into an opportunity for failure, and this inhibits personal growth.

- **Use Self-Talk**. Use positive self-talk as an opportunity to counter harmful assumptions. For example, when you catch yourself expecting perfection, remind yourself that you can't do everything perfectly, that it's only possible to try to do things your way and to try to do them well. This allows you to accept yourself as you are, while still striving to improve.

- **Self-Evaluate**. Learn to evaluate yourself independently and honestly. Doing so allows you to avoid the constant sense of turmoil that comes from relying exclusively on the opinions of others. Focusing internally and examining how you feel (your emotions), will give you a stronger sense of "self" and it will prevent you from giving your personal power away to others.

See yourself as the "self confident" person you want to be and before you know it you will become that person. If you have a setback don't let it get you down. Just remember the times when you exhibited self confidence (and how good it felt) and then try again. Each time you try it will help you to build confidence. Do this until 'confidence building' becomes a way of life.

It's Your Life, It's Your Choice

Choose Communication

"Take advantage of every opportunity to practice your communication skills so that when important occasions arise, you will have the gift, the style, the sharpness, the clarity, and the emotions to affect other people."

Jim Rohn

The purpose of communication is to get your message across to others clearly and unambiguously. Doing this involves effort from both the sender of the message and the receiver. And it's a process that can be fraught with error, with messages often misinterpreted by the recipient. When this isn't detected, it can cause tremendous confusion, wasted effort and missed opportunity. And most important, it can effect the decision making process.

In fact, communication is only successful when both the sender and the receiver understand the same information as a result of the communication. By successfully getting your message across, you convey your thoughts and ideas effectively. When not successful, the thoughts and ideas that you send do not necessarily reflect your own, causing a communications breakdown and creating roadblocks that stand in the way of your goals – both personally and professionally.

In spite of the increasing importance placed on communication skills, many individuals continue to struggle, unable to communicate their thoughts and ideas effectively – whether in verbal or written format. This inability makes it nearly impossible for them to compete effectively in life, and stands in the way of real achievement. Getting your message across is paramount to progressing. To do this, you must understand what your message is, what audience you are sending it to, and how it will be perceived.

Problems with communication can pop-up at every stage of the communication process and they have the potential to create misunderstanding and confusion.

To be an effective communicator and to get your point across without misunderstanding and confusion, your goal should be to develop clear, concise, accurate, well-planned communications within the home and the workplace.

Know how communication works

- Know that communication is a two-way process.

- Know how to listen to people, make them feel valued and involved, and know when it is important to focus on the individual rather than the group.

- Be aware of different ways of communicating, including electronic channels, and understand barriers to communication.

- Be aware that the child, young person, parent, friend or partner may not have understood what is being communicated.

Listen and build empathy

- Establish rapport and respectful, trusting relationships with everyone concerned.

- Be aware that some people do not communicate verbally very well and that you may need to adapt your style of communication to their needs and abilities.

- Understand the effects of non-verbal communication such as body language.

- Build open and honest relationships by respecting everyone and making them feel valued and appreciated.

- Actively listen in a calm, open, non-threatening manner and use questions to check understanding and acknowledge about what's been said.

Communicate for healthy relationships

Communication involves almost every aspect of our interactions with others; for this reason, communication and relationships are inseparably connected. You can't have a relationship with someone without communicating with them. Communication involves how we express our thoughts, ideas, and feelings to others, including what we say and how we say it. But when we communicate with others, we also communicate attitudes, values, priorities, and beliefs. No matter what we actually say to other people in words, we also send messages about what we think of them, what we think of ourselves, and whether or not we're being sincere and genuine in what we say. Our non-verbal communication – those things we don't say with words, but with our gestures, our facial expressions, and our attitude – speak volumes.

It's Two-Way Traffic

What we say and do, and how we say and do it, directly shapes how people experience us. In fact, many times, the opinions people form about us are based on the way we communicate. It also directly influences how they communicate in return. In other words, communication is a two way street. You may instigate or initiate a communication, but until you've received a response there has been no real communication.

Communicate in the Real World

Communication can be clear or vague, open or guarded, honest or dishonest – it can even be spoken or non-spoken – but there is no such thing as "non" communication. In fact, virtually everything we do in the company of others communicates something. Our body language, facial expressions, tone of voice, and level of interest (or disinterest) communicate something to the perceptive observer.

Because our ideas and interests are transmitted to other people through the way we communicate, we're more apt to get our needs met if we are effective communicators. The problem is that often we think we're communicating one thing but are actually communicating something quite different, or we're communicating so poorly that no one quite understands what it is we're trying to say.

Ineffective Communication

Ineffective communication is characterised by one or more the following elements:

- Indirect (doesn't get to the point, never clearly states purpose or intention),

- Passive (timid and reserved),

- Antagonistic (angry, aggressive, or hostile tone),

- Cryptic (underlying message or purpose is obscured and requires interpretation),

- Hidden (true agenda is never stated directly),

- Non-verbal (meaning is communicated through body language and behaviours, not words),

- One way (more talk than listening),

- Unresponsive (little interest in the perspective or needs of the other person),

- Off base (responses and needs of the other person are misunderstood and misinterpreted),

- Dishonest (dishonest statements are substituted for true feelings, thoughts, and needs),

Effective Communication

On the other hand, effective communication is:

- Direct (to-the-point, leaving no doubt as to meaning or purpose),

- Assertive (not afraid to state what is wanted or why),

- Congenial (affable and friendly),

- Clear (underlying issues are clear),

- Open (no intentionally hidden messages or meaning),

- Verbal (words are used to clearly express ideas),

- Two way (equal amounts of talking and listening),

- Responsive (attention paid to the needs and perspective of others),

- On Track (correctly interprets responses and needs of others),

- Honest (true feelings, thoughts, and expectations are stated),

Communicating in Important Relationships

Where there are many factors involved in healthy relationships, the ability to communicate effectively is one important route to mutual satisfaction within any relationship. Effective communication is an essential part of day-to-day life, and especially so in important relationships. Here is how you can improve your communication skills in this area:

- *Put a premium on openness.* Find ways to be honest, express your feelings, and share ideas.

- *Share your problems*. Sharing the good times and the bad times is important in relationships, and serves to deepen and strengthen relationships and communication within them.

- *Share your daily life*. Share those things in your life that are interesting, funny, sad, or affect you in some way. Find a way to connect with others, sharing your life with them and allowing them to share their lives with you.

- *Avoid verbally bruising other people*. Refrain from insults, put-downs, and expressions of disgust, and avoid generalisations which are not only stereotypes, but often hurt.

- *Boost self-esteem, don't crush it*. When it comes to relationship building, naming someone's deficiencies or failures is rarely as effective as praise. Focus on each other's positive traits. Find something good to say, catch each other doing something right, and help build self confidence and self esteem.

- *Avoid controlling*. Whenever one person seeks to always be right, always be the agenda-setter, and always be the virtuous one, he or she may feel like a winner – but it's the relationship that suffers.

"I like hearing myself talk. It is one of my greatest pleasures. I often have long conversations with myself, and I am so clever that sometimes I don't understand a single word of what I am saying."

Oscar Wilde

Choose Commitment

"There are only two options regarding commitment. You're either in or out. There's no such thing as a life in-between."

Pat Riley

In our 'fast-track' modern society, where everything is seen to be either disposable or dispensable, commitment is probably an ugly word. Today, it's far easier when something is broken, to throw it away and get a new one, than it is to fix it. However, if you desire to make your decisions "right" you will need to be committed to every task – whether it be in the home or workplace.

What is commitment

The most important single factor in any individual's success is commitment. Real commitment ignites action. To commit is to pledge yourself completely to a certain purpose or line of conduct. It also means practising your beliefs consistently. There are, therefore, two fundamental conditions for commitment.

The first is having a sound set of beliefs. The second is faithful adherence to those beliefs with your behaviour. Possibly the best description of commitment is "persistence with a purpose".

Where to practice commitment

It appears that achievers hold dearly to only a few commitments. The first, and most basic, of these is a commitment to a set of values, principles or beliefs (their own value system). These underlying principles define both the person's uniqueness and the primary direction in which he/she wants to head. This first commitment leads to a distinct vision and purpose in life. The second commitment is to oneself, to how one acts as an individual. An effective achiever possesses a strong sense of personal integrity and self confidence. This leads to a willingness to share the credit for success. Another side to this commitment is a deliberate emphasis on continual self-improvement. The combination of a strong, positive commitment to self, and to a set of principles, serve as a foundation to effectively maintaining all other commitments.

Balancing all your commitments is the key to a well directed personal life and career. But remember, a strong and healthy commitment to people is the glue that holds everything together. If you are afraid of commitment you actually stifle yourself and hinder your own achievements.

How to practice commitment

The irony of commitment is that it's deeply liberating – in work, in play, in love.

Anne Morriss

Effectively demonstrating commitment to others, to basic principles, and to oneself is never easy. The truth is, demonstrating commitment is hard work. Wavering commitment is usually seen as no commitment at all. The only way to achieve a reputation for commitment is through determination and persistence. Genuine commitment stands the test of time. Day to day, commitment is demonstrated by a combination of two actions.

The first action is called "supporting." Genuine support develops a commitment in the minds and hearts of others. This is accomplished by focusing on what is important and acting accordingly. It is not uncommon for people to be either confused as to what is important, or lose sight of it over time. Supporting means concentrating on what adds value, spotlighting what's working, and rewarding yourself and others who are focusing on what is important.

A crucial aspect of true support is standing up to those who would undermine your commitment, those whose words or actions show disrespect.

The second action underlying commitment is called "improving." Improving stretches our commitment to an even higher level. Commitment means a willingness to look for a better way and learn from the process. It focuses on eliminating complacency, confronting what is not working, and providing incentives for improvement. The spirit of improving is rooted in challenging current expectation and ultimately taking the risk to make changes. These changes are based more on optimism for the future rather than dissatisfaction with the past.

It is the combination of both supporting and improving behaviours that makes up the practice of commitment. Separately neither action is capable of sustaining commitment, but together they provide a needed balance. Both are essential to commitment at any level.

When it is most important

Commitment is most difficult and most readily proven during tough times. How someone weathers the storms most clearly demonstrates their basic beliefs. Epicurus stated: *"...A captain earns his reputation during the storms."* When the opposition scores big against you, when the money dries up, or when the glamour of success wears off, this is when it is easiest to compromise your commitments. The real test comes when you can hold the line against the easy route of compromise.

Fortunately, paying the price that commitment commands has payoffs worth the cost – a reputation for integrity and, even more important, the commitment of others in return. Commitment is a two-way street. You only get it if you are willing to give it – especially in personal relationships.

Commitment in a relationship

The question of when a relationship is committed is a source of much confusion and debate. We live in a time when the marriage rate is going down, the cohabitation rate is going up, and the majority of first-born children are now born to unmarried parents. This is why so many couples and individuals are challenged by different perceptions of the status of their relationships. But the truth is, with no one willing to give any commitment in a relationship, the future is unsure and insecure. This brings about a lack of security and produces dysfunctional behaviour. We all have a need to belong, and this need for belonging must be satisfied. In a relationship, commitment does exactly that!

A commitment is explicit and unambiguous. A commitment is a formal event of some kind between two people. A commitment is something you do over time. A real commitment is usually legally enforceable and there are consequences for breaking it. And, for a relationship to be truly committed, there are no exit doors – mentally, emotionally, or physically. When the going gets rough, you make it work.

Commitments versus Promise

Promise: Verbally stated future intention to perform a specific act.

- I promise to pick up your dry cleaning and not forget this time.

- I promise to be faithful in our relationship.

Commitment: A recognisable fact demonstrated by behaviour; and an attitude consisting of thoughts and beliefs.

- I am committed to keeping my promises.

    -    I am committed to our relationship.

In short, a promise is something you say, and a commitment is something you do. A promise is situation-specific. A commitment is contextual. A promise is a small commitment. If a potential partner doesn't keep promises, I would question their ability to keep commitments, as they are definitely related. Commitment is not a light switch that goes from "off" to "on." When building a relationship with someone, the level of commitment gradually increases. Working with this assumption, your commitment level today should be more than it was yesterday!

Fear of commitment

Fear of commitment makes it hard for you to decide on whatever you need to decide on especially if the future's at stake. Therefore, having a fear of commitment is not healthy at all. It can really hold you back because you must be able to make the most of opportunities that come your way, but it can be defeated. Fear of commitment scientifically, is a type of phobia. It refers to a person who is afraid of being committed to any deep relationships, tasks, projects or responsibilities.

Fear of commitment can be triggered by various causes. Fear of commitment may start from childhood when a person suffered from a traumatic experience, such as separation of parents, divorce, or death. Fear of commitment can also be a result of poor role models in which the person may have witnessed offensive relationships. And even worse, the person may have been a victim of it. These experiences have a great impact on the person's decision making, and are the cause of the development of their fear of commitment.

When repairing our relationships we should take some time to reflect on fear, and the possible confusion about commitment. We each require companionship, challenges, creative fulfilment and love.

But it seems that we keep ourselves separate, create imaginary differences between each other from a sense of fear. Maybe a fear of commitment? In my experience, if we make the choice to accept that we really aren't that dissimilar to each other, this fear dissolves.

Choose Contentment

True contentment is a thing as active as agriculture. It is the power of getting out of any situation all that there is in it. It is arduous and it is rare.

Gilbert K. Chesterton

My personal definition of contentment is – the ability to remain happy in any circumstance due to the belief that everything is subject to change for the better. The Greek word translated "contentment" is "autarkeia" which means *"a perfect condition of life in which no aid or support is needed."* Therefore, contentment comes, not because of a passive acceptance of whatever our condition may be, but because there is a *"perfect condition of life in which no aid or support is needed"* – inasmuch as every one of us already possess whatever he/she needs to face life and conquer it! An interesting and inspiring thought.

Happiness is a quality decision you choose to make

The most basic description of contentment I could find is; *"happy with my situation in life."*

But happiness is a choice. When you get up each morning you can choose to be happy or you can choose to be miserable and dissatisfied with everything. It's entirely up to you. Happiness is a quality decision you choose to make, not an emotion you feel. If you are constantly listening to your emotions you will never stay "up." You must make up your mind that you are going to be happy, in spite of your emotions. Many of us live in constant turmoil. We're always upset at something or other; or we are always frustrated at not getting the results we desire, but our happiness is just a decision away. It's as close to us as our thoughts are!

Scientific research agrees that one of the healthiest things you can do is laugh. So why not start by deciding to smile more often. You may be going through some tough times, and feel that you have good reason to be unhappy. Yet, being unhappy won't change anything. Learn to laugh in the face of defeat, and in the face of potential disaster. This way, you prepare yourself for victory.

With the right mental attitude, it doesn't matter what you may be going through, or how difficult it may seem, you can come through it. But you must stand, and remain standing. I believe it's more important to stay standing-up on the inside. It may take courage and determination, however, you can do it if you decide to do so. Yes, you can develop a winner's mentality, and apply it in every situation.

Some people may be thinking, *"I don't know what's been wrong with me. I've lost my drive and my enthusiasm. I now feel like I'm just going through the motions."* Well, believe me, regardless of your stressful situation, your financial status, past failures or how you're feeling – you can remain "up." Start by building a positive picture of yourself. How you view yourself, your personality and character, and your own accomplishments will determine your real sense of self-worth and self-value.

Low self-esteem breeds low enthusiasm, and in turn, it brings about a loss of drive and produces much frustration. Such an attitude will keep you down and keep you bound up in negativity.

Unless you have a positive picture of yourself no one else can see it or enjoy it. Others will always see you as you see yourself. Sometimes happiness is simply feeling good about yourself.

Strengthen your strengths

Over time, parents, schooling, work mates and friends may have conditioned you to think a certain way and many of you are now failure conscious. Consequently, you have become more problem-oriented than you are possibility-oriented. You instinctively focus on your weaknesses and have lost confidence and self-respect. However, if you learn to manage around your weaknesses and strengthen your strengths, you will discover a lot of "plus factors" that you didn't know you had. This can start a reversal away from negative attitudes and steer you toward positive self-belief and contentment.

You will never rise above the image you have of yourself. Therefore, stop looking at your lacks, frailties and weaknesses and be thankful for all the skills and talents you have. Be thankful for the natural gifts and abilities that you possess – no matter how undeveloped they are. This way you will focus on them all the more and produce a clear picture of the "successful you". Seeing yourself as being successful will keep your enthusiasm levels high. But you must keep your thought life in check. And remember, you can only move away from a bad thought by deliberately moving toward a good one.

What is your self-image? Who do you think you are? These are important questions that demand an answer. Why? Because a healthy self-image is one of the key factors in establishing success and happiness. You are only able to speak, act and react as the person you think you are. Low self-esteem means a low level of motivation, and low motivation cannot pick you up, or keep you up. To be up all the time you must generate enough energy through happiness and enthusiasm.

Far too many people have a defeatist attitude, they are quick to wave the white flag of surrender every time they encounter opposition. Winners are always 'up' on the inside. They see every negative situation as being subject to change (for the better). They see all things working together for their good, and as a result, they are content.

You may be going through a dark time in life. Perhaps someone has let you down badly, or taken advantage of you, or even mistreated you, and you're tempted to sit around and have a pity party. Well, stand up on the inside! Change your mental attitude. Sitting around mopping all day will not change your circumstances. Some people have made up their minds to be happy, but only after their circumstances have changed. Only then will they have a good attitude, only then will they get up on the inside.

Practice self-encouragement

Getting up on the inside is part of the process of making yourself strong – it is self-encouragement in the midst of emotional turmoil. Getting up and doing something to encourage yourself may be the very thing that secures your breakthrough. But before you can do anything, you may need to examine yourself closely. Many times we view negative circumstances in our lives as being the result of an external intrusion. We start speaking to the problems 'out there', not realising that the problem may be inside of us. Self examination is the process by which you weed out all that's choking your future. If you have any hurts or unforgiveness, deal with them as quickly as possible. You can't encourage yourself with deep rooted negative feelings present.

After you have 'stood up on the inside', make a quality decision to live a happy and contented life. In our daily lives, we often rush through tasks, trying to get them done, trying to finish as much as we can each day, speeding along in our cars to our next destination, rushing to do what we need to do there, and then leaving so that we can speed to our next destination. At the end of the day, we're often exhausted and stressed out from the grind and the chaos and the busyness of the day.

We don't have time for what's important to us, for what we really want to be doing – for spending time with loved ones, for doing things we're passionate about. And yet, it doesn't have to be that way. It's possible to live a simpler life, one where you enjoy each activity, where you are relaxed in everything (or most things) you do, where you are content rather than frantically rushing to finish things.

How to live a peaceful, uncluttered life

If this appeals to you, let's take a look at some suggestions for living an uncluttered, peaceful, and contented life:

1. **Decide what's important**. First, take a step back and think about what's important to you. What do you really want to be doing, who do you want to spend your time with, what do you want to accomplish with your work? Make a short list of things you would like to add to your life; people you want to spend time with; and things you'd like to accomplish at home or at work.

2. **Examine your commitments**. A big part of the problem is that our lives are way too full. We can't possibly do everything we have committed to doing, and we certainly can't enjoy it if we're trying to do everything. Accept that you can't do everything. Decide that you want to do what's important to you, and try to eliminate the commitments that aren't as important.

3. **Do less each day**. Don't fill your day up with things to do. You will end up rushing to do them all. If you normally try (and fail) to do 7-10 things, do 3 important ones instead (with 3 more smaller items to do if you get those three done). This will give you time to do what you need to do, and not rush.

4. **Create time for solitude**. In addition to slowing down and enjoying the tasks you do, and then doing less of them, it's also important to just have some time to yourself. You need time to relax, reflect and let your mind wander.

5. **Do nothing**. Sometimes, it's good to forget about doing things, and do absolutely nothing. Doing nothing is fine! So don't allow yourself to feel

guilty. In fact, when you do nothing and take your mind off the issues at hand, you'll probably get all the right answers.

6. **Sprinkle simple pleasures throughout your day**. Knowing what your simple pleasures are, and strategically placing a few of them into each day, can go a long way to making life more pleasurable.

7. **Do only what you enjoy doing**. This is so important, because it quickly de-stresses your life. Every day should be enjoyed – not endured! So select the things you enjoy doing, and wherever possible, remove the things you don't like doing.

Success is not the key to happiness. Happiness is the key to success. If you love what you are doing, you will be successful.

Albert Schweitzer

Conclusion

"You can begin right now to act as if you have achieved any goal you desire."

Jack Canfield

If you have read through to this part of the book, by now you will probably know that making right choices is not that simple. There is no quick fix! But don't be concerned or get discouraged, it is possible to get the results you desire. You don't have to apply every principle and fundamental law at the same time. Start by using the one you feel needs to operate in your life right now. If you think that accepting change and raising your level of commitment are priorities, choose to make these adjustments immediately. And it's the same with the character traits.

Embrace change and start to become the person you would like to be by strengthening your weakest personal qualities. For instance, if you are indecisive or undisciplined start building these qualities first.

I have been teaching many of these universal laws or principles for over a decade. Most of these topics have been covered in my sermons, but from a Christian perspective. However, this doesn't make them less effective. In fact, I only serve up what I myself have partaken of. Therefore, it is experiential knowledge that I use whether teaching or preaching. Be rest assured, I have lived this book, and will continue to live as much of it as is necessary, because I know it works. This is why I am encouraging you to start putting it into practice.

Begin Right Now!

There is nothing more exciting than spontaneity. Living in the "now" and enjoying every moment is precious. Most people never learn to appreciate what they have right where they are! Theodore Roosevelt once said, "Do what you can, with what you have, right where you are." Where do you begin? You begin where you are right now. Doing what you can, with what you have! I am of the opinion that when we use what we've got in our hands, we are able to obtain what we have in our hearts. Our innermost desires become a reality. Therefore, you must look inside, think, decide and then take action! Your heartfelt dreams and expectations can be yours. They are within your reach!

What matters more than anything is that you take immediate action on something you have discovered while reading this book – something you believe may assist you achieve your goals. Not every line you've read has jumped off the page and grabbed your attention. However, there were probably chapters or passages that you could relate to, or you felt could help you with a situation you are currently facing. Maybe something mentioned has even touched your heart. So, don't delay or procrastinate. If you think any of the principles outlined in this book can improve your life, work, or personal effectiveness – then do something now! Make a positive decision to choose action. The results will astound you.

Why not begin today by deciding exactly what you want in life. Write out a "shopping list" of everything you would like to achieve – things that you know will make you happy and contented. However, when doing this exercise, try not to be cautious or conservative. Take the lid off! Dream big dreams! There are really no limits on what you can accomplish except for the limits you place on yourself by the way you think. So set your goals high and let everything you plan have a hint of the impossible. Be more creative, and get accustomed to meditating on things that truly excite and inspire you. And only do what you enjoy doing. Stir up your expectations and start to make quality decisions (and wise choices) based on the things you've learnt in this book.

Note, the different "choices" laid out in Part Two, and those "key attributes" I've encouraged you to adopt in Part One, are in fact all intertwined. They are like a tapestry of different colours, textures and patterns. Put together and applied correctly they will enhance your life, build character and benefit your relationships. As you learn to recognise, understand and then use them, you will frame your future with success and fill your life with happiness. Remember what was mentioned earlier – these universal principles are like phone numbers, every time you dial the number you should make the same connection. There is nothing random about it, and that is why it's so exciting – it works every time!

You are special, and someone as special as you deserves to live a life that's out of the ordinary. I love what Jesus said, "I have come that you may have life, and have life super-abundantly." I pray that you find the super-abundant life that Jesus talked about.

About the Author - Chris Demetriou

The world around us is permeated with expectations. Each individual's expectations will have a profound effect, not only on themselves, but also on the people around them.

Chris Demetriou

Chris was born in Phiti a little village in Cyprus. He was raised in South Africa but has spent most of his professional life in the United Kingdom. He started work as a musician and attained considerable success as a songwriter and record producer. One of his songs "Step On" appears in Q magazine's top hundred singles of all time, and the original version "He's Gonna Step On You Again" was eventually cited by The Guinness Book of Records as being the first sample ever used on a record (it also made the Billboard Hot 100 twice and the Daily Mail's list of the "500 Greatest Songs Ever").

Chris' diverse career, spanning three decades, reflects a unique ability to make things happen. As an entrepreneur, his past and present ventures include; Chestnut Productions (record production and music publishing), The Connaught Group (sports sponsorship and management), Demco (public relations), Promise Productions (mail order), Avalon Services (financial services), ACTS International Corp. (media brokerage and rights acquisition), New Africa Networks (terrestrial broadcast network), ShowRights (entertainment exchange portal) and Emba Media Management (media acquisition).

Chris is Founder and Senior Pastor of Cornerstone Ministries, a church and charity situated in Esher, Surrey, England. The church services are filmed and broadcast weekly on Life Matters TV, and the website has over 100 thousand page requests each month. His sermon notes are extremely popular and a large number people regularly listen to his Podcasts on iTunes. His unique humour, personable delivery and insightful knowledge of the original Greek has made him a sought-after speaker. Chris' practical approach to helping individuals navigate the storms of life has impacted many thousands. However, his prominent gift is the ability to process, filter and simplify universal laws. He is passionate and loves to expound on Biblical Principles that contain the timeless wisdom he has been able to discover and put into practice. He is insightful, intuitive, discerning, and his excellent communication and interpersonal skills have made him successful both in ministry and business. Chris has owned his own TV Network, and for many years he has run a successful Media Brokerage firm. Presently he controls the world's forth largest children's animation library. His professional history in music and media spans thirty years and incorporates multiple areas of business activity. This is his second book.

Chris is a professional member of the Performing Rights Society; a full member of the British Association of Songwriters, Composers and Authors; an associate member of the Institute of Marketing Managers; and a member of the International Federation of Christian Churches.

More information can be found in Wikipedia under his full name Christos Demetriou.

www.ingramcontent.com/pod-product-compliance
Lightning Source LLC
Chambersburg PA
CBHW030418100426
42812CB00028B/3005/J